When the
Stars
Fall
Down

May God bless you,
in all ways always!

Pat Lamb

When the Stars Fall Down

*A Young Couple's
Journey in Following
God's Leadership
to Serve Others*

PAT LAMB

TATE PUBLISHING
AND ENTERPRISES, LLC

7008

Published by Tate Publishing & Enterprises, LLC
127 E. Trade Center Terrace | Mustang, Oklahoma 73064 USA
1.888.361.9473 | www.tatepublishing.com

Tate Publishing is committed to excellence in the publishing industry. The company reflects the philosophy established by the founders, based on Psalm 68:11,
"The Lord gave the word and great was the company of those who published it."

Book design copyright © 2013 by Tate Publishing, LLC. All rights reserved.
Cover design by Rodrigo Adolfo
Interior design by Caypeeline Casas

Published in the United States of America

ISBN: 978-1-62510-152-5
1. Biography & Autobiography / General
2. Biography & Autobiography / Religious
13.07.19

Dedication

To those who may be hesitant to step out in faith to follow our master's call and to those who have already done so, but who may feel that they are accomplishing little or nothing. To everyone, for the purpose of inspiring praise to our God for keeping His promises.

Acknowledgements

*M*ost of all, I am grateful for my Lord and Savior for His faithfulness in keeping those who put their trust in Him. I can truly say as the song says, "Jesus Led Me all the Way."

I owe much to our oldest son, Kenneth, for being my personal computer consultant! He has been very patient with me with all of my questions.

Our daughter, Trish Poe, has been my enthusiastic cheerleader throughout my endeavors and has helped me tremendously.

Our youngest son, Charles, has stood by me in support of my ideas. His wife, Kelly, has been of help with the computer and with ideas.

Our grandchildren, Dylan and LeAndra Nelson, have lavished their love and respect for Nana and Grandpa through the years and have been great blessings.

Our grandchildren, Garrett and Spencer, have truly been rays of sunshine in our older years.

Our second son, David, who is no longer with us, continued to prod and encourage me to write even from my first book *Let the Children Come* and through the writing of my second book *Children, Come to Me*. He had dreamed of writing that "big poem" that would be published. He was a gifted creative writer and reviewed some of the writing for this book and made suggestions. Two of his poems are included in this book.

People along the paths we have traveled have taught much to my husband and me, and we are grateful.

Table of Contents

Introduction

This book is the story of a young girl who decided to give her life to Christ and tried her best to follow His guidance. This autobiography demonstrates how God led her step by step to several different places, allowed her to meet many different people, and provided a husband who joined in her efforts to follow God's guidance. Everyone has a story because God works in each life to fulfill His plan. The author has chosen to tell this story with the hope that it may serve as an encouragement to others to yield to God's calling.

The spellings of Navajo words in this book are the author's own spellings as she recalls the words being pronounced. The Navajo language is a descriptive language and not root-word based, making it one of the most difficult languages to learn. Since the Navajo reservation is so large, there are several dialects in the language, making it very complicated indeed.

Whispers in the Wind

The chilling wind whistles and howls as it blows.
Where did it start? No one knows where it goes.
Does it carry with it all the words spoken so clear?
Does it then drop them in an unsuspecting heart so dear?

᰾

Does the wind drop those words as seeds meant to grow?
Or does it fling them afar so none will ever know
Of the wisdom, advice, lovingly given to those
Whose need was felt for a life of repose.

᰾

Well intentioned are those who would freely advise
People less fortunate and so much less wise.
Yet one has to wonder if any good was done
Has anyone really been helped…even one?

᰾

Has all effort been snatched up as whispers in wind,
Or has something really stuck as with others they blend?

Wonderful it is that we're not judged on results,
But effort and heart are what God sees in us.

What joy to serve such a loving God and Son
With faith to obey, hoping for a soul to be won.
We will know happiness at its very best
When our work is done and we go to our rest.

It is not for us to wonder and ponder and pine
The will of our Lord, so very divine.
As we journey through life and we trust and obey,
We eventually learn there is no better way.

&

Whether whispers in the wind or shouts from on high
All that matters is that God is nigh.
It is He who makes wind, man, thoughts, and all other
So we simply love Him, His Son, and our brother.

—Pat Lamb

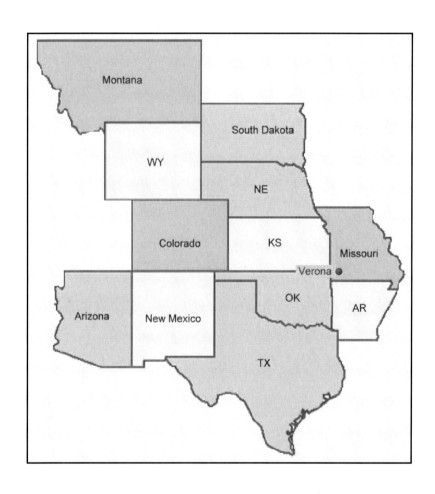

A Great Place to Start

*V*erona is a small town, but a big blessing to many folks who have been fortunate enough to have lived there for even a short time. It was thoughtfully located near the head of the Spring River in the beautiful Ozarks in Southwest Missouri, and inhabited by mostly Italian immigrants who came to America to escape persecution in the old country. Most of the original settlers, Waldensian Presbyterians, moved on to Monett where farmland was flatter and better, but other folks came and started the first Sunday school west of the Mississippi River, built the old red mill, and saw that the railroad came and ran right smack-dab through the valley. A few store buildings were built parallel to the railroad about a block away. One could look across the railroad tracks and see beautiful rolling hills that were situated alongside the river. Before the town was built, the Indian folks had recognized the importance of this location as evidenced by the many arrowheads found along the river and the mounds where teepees had rested, still faintly evident in some of the fields. Collections of those arrowheads can be seen in the museum at the College of the Ozarks in Hollister, Missouri, even today.

Verona never grew to be a big town. All the time I lived there, a sign on both sides of Verona on Highway 60 declared that the population was 405. This population supported at least four churches as evidence to the fact that the small town was populated by God-fearing people, albeit there may have been a few differences in beliefs as to what God directed the folks to do.

The most active churches were the Catholic and Baptist. The Catholic church even had a school where the nuns dogmatically saw to it that the kids behaved and did their lessons. They were threatening enough just to look at as they would occasionally stroll downtown in their black habits and starched white collars to pick up a few items from the stores, but to the kids who went to the school, they were third in line to God right after the priest. Located between the Catholic and Baptist churches, that were only about a block and a half apart, was an empty old-time-looking brick church that had once housed the Presbyterians. It had a smaller steeple than the Catholic church had, but one could easily tell that it had been elegant and stately in its time by the beautiful stained glass windows. The white framed Christian church sat about a block from the Catholic church in another direction. That was where most of the school staff attended. Then, when I was in junior high, the empty church building a couple of blocks on the other side of the Catholic church became the home of the Independent Fundamental Methodist Church. Moreover, several country churches were scattered around outside the town limits within a few miles driving distance.

The Catholic church had a tall steeple and beautiful bells that rang two times each day as if to remind all that time is important and shouldn't be wasted. It was said that people came from as far as Pierce City just to hear those bells. Pierce City is about twenty miles away! Toward the top of the steeple was the outline of a rectangle, no doubt a door to get inside to make repairs to the bells. My sister, Wanda, would not miss the opportunity to frighten my younger sister, Rosemary, and me by telling us that it was a trap door. "If you don't behave," she said, "the priest will come and get you and take you up there and throw you out that trap door!" Undoubtedly, this helped a great deal when she took care of us while our folks were busy.

The Baptist church was a bustling church with people so friendly that they waved at everybody whether they knew them or not. Every summer, the kind Baptist ladies worked hard in Vacation Bible School to provide learning activities for all the children they could round up. The Baptist church building was an unimposing white, wooden structure on a corner up the street from the more expensively built brick church building once used by the Presbyterians. Since hardly any buildings were ever locked, some of my friends and I used to go into the old Presbyterian church and tried to play the organ on occasion.

The street that ran through town headed directly for a small park before turning a sharp curve to go on to Aurora. In the center of the park was a concrete statue of a World War I soldier, who is still standing at attention today, displaying a list of patriotic Verona citizens who had fought and died in that war. That statue instilled no small amount of patriotism in Verona's children as they played in the park. It stood as a testimony not only to the deep love of country shown by those who had given the ultimate, but the deep inner love of Verona's citizens for country. The Spring River Cemetery located near the head of Spring River gave further testimony to that fact when one looked at the many small grave markers of Civil War heroes. To the soldier's right and up the hill was the school for grades 1–12, where I spent all twelve school years. Going back downtown, one could find three grocery stores, a post office, a drug store, mechanic garage, beer joint, Ely Walker factory, and a fire station. The fire station sounded the siren every day at six o'clock right after the bells rang at the Catholic church as if to say, "That's right! You'd better pay attention to time! It's passing fast!" As the siren screamed, dogs all across town and the countryside, as far as it could be heard, howled and barked their displeasure. Everyone who could afford a watch checked to see if it was accurate. They would touch the stem, and if needed, wind it a few cranks to keep it going another day.

There was only one doctor in town, and he lived and worked in a two-story white house. The house also served as a hospital. It was this doctor who got a call from my dad one night that mom was about to deliver a baby. The doctor jumped in his vehicle, drove across Spring River and up Roder Hill (named after the people who lived at the top of the hill). He then went down and up two more hills until he turned right on a gravel lane to our house that was about two miles out from town. It was that night that I was born, October 19, 1936, during the Great Depression. To this day, I can't help but feel a little guilt when I hear that record heat temperatures were set that summer while my mom was carrying me. Of course, there was no air conditioning at that time, and my mom was still cooking on a wood stove!

I was welcomed by three older sisters, Ernestine, Wanda, and Helene. Rosemary was to make her debut into the world almost two years later. After my dad had five girls, he gave up trying to have a son. Ernestine was ten years old at the time, Wanda was six years old, and Helene was four.

Our family owned a grocery store. It had an adjoining wall to the Lechner grocery store that made for a friendly business competition between the two. I remember watching Mr. Lechner get in his little red pickup, load up groceries, and start his delivery service around town. It seemed that he did that about the same time every afternoon. If one happened to pass the Catholic church a few minutes after he left, the little red pickup would be seen parked there while Mr. Lechner went in and said his prayers. When his little six-year-old son began losing his teeth, my dad started calling Clarence "Snaggletooth." This nickname was later shortened to Snags, and that is the name he goes by to this day. Little Snags married my sister Wanda right out of high school. People forgot his real name, and when he had back surgery several years later, the Aurora radio station announced the condition of Snags Lechner every hour or so.

Across the street from the grocery stores was the Ely Walker Fixture Factory. At noon and break time, the workers would pour out of the building and come to our restaurant in the back of the store for fresh baked pie and coffee or perhaps a bowl of chili. My mom and Mrs. Buehler did all the cooking. When the factory closed, the restaurant closed as well, but while we ran the restaurant, we sure ate well.

Our family truck was a three-fourth-ton truck that served many purposes including hauling cattle, delivering groceries, or transporting us. The bed of the truck had removable wooden ingates for hauling cattle or a covered boxlike structure built by my dad for delivering groceries. Every morning, after the cows were milked, we would all pile into my dad's old red truck and head for town. All five of us girls would ride in the back, when weather permitted, singing at the top of our voices across the country and into town. I'm sure everyone enjoyed hearing "You are my Sunshine," "Home on the Range," "She'll be Comin' Round the Mountain," and other favorites. We must have been a sight to see! We would always argue about who got to stand up front in the corners with a foot on the second board of the ingates facing the wind. We loved to feel the wind blowing in our face and through our hair.

When we finally got to town, we could choose almost anything for our breakfast as Mrs. Buehler would already be there mixing up her pie dough and crumbling up her brick chili. Lots of times, I would have a glass of milk with a sliced banana and cookies crumbled up in it. This was delicious until one morning, Mrs. Buehler said, "Patsy, that doesn't look good!" After her comment, I made other choices.

In addition to having five girls to care for, when my dad's mom had passed away, she left four of my dad's brothers for mom and daddy to take in. My mom told me in her later days that she could remember going to the chicken house and sitting on a tomato crate, putting her head in her hands, and crying because she didn't know what she would fix for everyone to eat. We ate lots of beans, fried potatoes, and cornbread. We always had a garden in the summer, and when fall came, my dad and neighbors usually butchered a hog. They would spread the fresh meat on a table covered with oil cloth on the screened-in back porch and preserve it with hickory-flavored salt. Our cows provided dairy products for consumption. My mom was adept at wringing the head off a chicken and preparing it to eat. Ernestine said that if a car turned down the lane, mom would yell and tell her to put some water on to boil. Mom would grab a chicken, wring its head off, and by the time the car got there she would be in the process of plucking its feathers. Despite hard times and limited food supplies, she would tell our guests, "You'll have to stay for dinner! I was just fixin' a chicken!"

Ernestine worked very hard helping mom with the housework. Wanda worked hard at babysitting and playing pranks on the rest of us. Helene worked hard at defending herself and making her wants known, and I worked hard at being the boy my dad had always wanted and given up on having. Rosemary—well—Rosemary was the baby. She pitched in here and there as needed. We all had to do much more than most children have to do nowadays. Years later, I told my mom that I had always felt that she favored Rosemary over me. I was hoping for my mom to reassure me that I was wrong. Her reply was, "Well, everybody favors the baby. She is the youngest!"

As was common at the time, raising children was a joint effort of the parents and older siblings in many families. My sisters had almost as much influence on me as my mom and dad. Everyone worked at whatever they could do to help the family survive. Mom often remarked that she was sure glad that I was a good baby because her time was so limited to care for me. My older sisters didn't seem to mind the chore of watching over Rosemary and me. They enjoyed telling stories and teasing us.

One of the ways my older sisters enjoyed teasing us was to sing "Babes in the Woods." The song always made us cry out of pity for the little babes. On one occasion, Rosemary and I decided to hide while they were singing. We had a snowball bush, and a spirea bush. We would go from one bush to another trying to hide from them, but they would follow us and sing the haunting lyrics. As I recall, the lyrics were:

Oh, don't you remember a long time ago
Two poor little babes whose names I don't know
Were stolen away one bright summer day
And left in the woods as I've heard people say?

They sobbed and they sighed
And they bitterly cried
And the poor little babes
Just lay down and died.

And when they were dead, the robins so red
Brought strawberry leaves and over them spread.
And all the day long they sang them this song,
Poor babes in the woods, poor babes in the woods.

—Author unknown

This is an old Ozark song. Although some might question the wisdom of singing such a sad song to children, I know now that it helped to develop compassion in us.

One night, two of my three older sisters and I were stretched crosswise on the bed in our little farmhouse looking out the window up at the stars. Since we didn't have electricity yet, and still used the dim light of oil lamps, you could see the stars from inside the house. By now, I was probably four or five years old. I just remember that I had not yet started to school. "Where did the stars come from?" I asked. This was a normal question for a preschooler, but the answer that followed has surprised many who have heard my story. My sister, Wanda, quickly answered, "God made them, and someday, they are all going to come crashing down, and the world is going to burn up, and everybody who isn't saved is going to hell!"

Now, many would debate the wisdom of this answer, but there is no denying that it provided the motivation for me to start trying to get saved. I'm sure she was just trying to scare me, as sisters sometimes do, but I began asking my mom and dad how I could get saved. My mom did not like to talk about religion. At that time, my dad didn't seem to want to talk about it either. I don't remember how I found out that I had to repent, believe that Jesus died on the cross, and invite him into my heart. Somehow, I got the idea that I had to also be willing to be a missionary. I kept trying to pray and kept asking God to save me.

With the limited amount of information I had gleaned, one Saturday night, I knelt by the bed in the back bedroom. I cried and told God I was sorry for the things I had done wrong, and if he wanted me to go to Africa or anyplace else when I grew up, I would do it. I expressed my belief in Jesus dying on the cross and asked to be saved.

There is no way I can completely describe what happened. I felt a burning sensation from head to toe and knew that the Holy Spirit had come to live in my heart. I went running into the living room where my mom was lying on the couch listening to the *Grand Ole Opry* on the battery operated radio. This was a Saturday night ritual for my mom. "Mom, I'm saved! I'm saved!" I shouted in utter exuberance. She put her finger to her mouth and said, "Shhh." She was listening to Ernest Tubb sing, "I'm Walkin' the Floor over You," and didn't want to be bothered.

I have never doubted my salvation since that night. I had not yet started first grade, but God looked down and saw that little girl and miraculously saved her. I can honestly say that even though I have made mistakes in my service to our Father, I have always tried to do the right thing and live up to what I believed he wanted me to do.

Since my family did not attend church, it wasn't easy to learn about what I was to do next. During my elementary school years,

I looked for every opportunity to find out more about church and God. The First Baptist Church ladies had Sunbeams in their homes after school in the afternoons. I can remember how pleasant it was to walk with a group of children to a nearby home in Verona. We were always greeted with smiles and smells of freshly baked cookies. Knowing how hungry we were after school, they would also have sandwiches. We would take our pennies or nickels as offering for the missionaries. We would sing songs about Jesus and hear a missionary story. Then, we would say a prayer for a missionary and go home with a good feeling inside. Attending Sunbeams and an occasional Vacation Bible School in the summer was the only religious teaching I experienced before I entered junior high when my family started attending church. One exception, however, was a revival someone talked my dad into attending at the Baptist church.

Daddy was a serious, hardworking man as many people had to be at that time. It was not easy to raise five daughters. Even though his brothers had left the home and were out on their own by the time I came along, they would need a little help occasionally. The people at the Baptist church kept inviting my family, and finally, my dad decided he would go to a revival. I listened intently, and when the invitation was given, I tugged on my dad's overalls and begged to go forward. He told me that I was too young to know what I was doing.

It was not until the little Independent Fundamental Methodist Church started that my dad decided our family should attend church. The little church was composed of a few folks who had broken away from the Baptist church because they felt the Baptists were too liberal. After all, some people in the Baptist church smoked cigarettes! By this time, I was in the seventh grade, and Ernestine and Wanda had already gotten married. I loved that little church! There were only four or five families who attended. One family had two little preschool boys, and I was asked to teach them. The little church building had a balcony in the back, and I would take them up there to tell them a Bible story. Then, they would get on their knees and use the bench for a table to color a picture. Every Sunday, I would get ready for church early and go sit in the car to wait for the others. While I was waiting, I would study my lesson, so I could do a good job teaching.

There was no one in the congregation who could play the piano. We had a piano at home, and Ernestine and Wanda had offered to pay for piano lessons for one summer if I were willing to walk the two miles to town. The first song I learned to play was "The Old Rugged Cross," and we sang that song every Sunday until I also learned "What a Friend we Have in Jesus." Next, I learned to play "Kneel at the Cross". For many Sundays, we sang those three songs. I gradually added more songs to my repertoire and continued playing for the church.

In addition to teaching and playing the piano, I was voted in as Sunday school treasurer. Every Sunday, I took the money home, counted it, and recorded it. During the coming week, Mom would take me to the bank in Aurora to deposit it. (That bank is now a restaurant!) I was once asked to lead the Bible study on a Wednesday night. I was also asked to plan the upcoming Christmas program. It was a simple program. I just read the story from the book of Luke, and at appropriate times, the congregation would sing the appropriate Christmas carol.

Our youth leader was a farmer and our neighbor. The thought never occurred to us that we needed a young man as our leader. He was about the same age as my dad. Every Sunday evening, he would give us a Bible drill using verses he had thoughtfully chosen for us to know. He always had us discuss what the verses meant. We could feel his love and care, and we loved him in return.

I was really happy in the Independent Fundamental Methodist Church, but my grandfather was a Pentecostal preacher, and my dad had been raised in that faith. Daddy decided he wanted to go to a Pentecostal church in Monett. My later high school years were spent going to church with my dad with no active part in the church.

My mom, being a faithful wife and mother, went with us except on Sunday mornings. Mom always stayed home on Sunday mornings to fix a big Sunday dinner. My three older sisters had married by that time, and their families came home each Sunday. We enjoyed those big dinners together. Those were such special times! Two of my brothers-in-law played on a baseball team in Aurora. After dinner, we would sometimes go to watch them play other whoever-we-can-get-to-play teams from Crane or other surrounding towns. When there was no game, we would sometimes cut a watermelon or make a freezer of ice cream after dinner later in the afternoon.

In the effort to follow my Lord, I tried to do my best in school. In first grade, I decided that when I graduated from high school, I wanted to be the valedictorian. We had eighth grade graduation, as well, and I was valedictorian of the eighth grade. Of course, the classes were very small. There were nineteen students in our high school graduating class, and I actually was the valedictorian.

In spite of its small size, Verona Schools did a good job educating the young people. There have been college teachers and even a state senator who graduated there. One of the Missouri state school superintendents went to school in Verona. The school system was different in many ways from most of today's schools. First, second, and third grades were all in one classroom. Miss Mary had everything perfectly organized. While she was having reading group with one grade, the other grades would be reading their story at their desks. Another student and I got to "tell words." Whenever a child didn't know a word, the child would raise a hand, and we would go tell what the word was. We had things to copy from the chalkboard for our writing. We started with cursive writing but never learned to print. At recess or during lunch time, Miss Mary would put problems on the board for us to work. We had to copy all the problems and write the answers.

Someone came and tested the eyes of all students. Miss Mary told my dad that I had bad eyes. He refused to believe that one of his daughters could have weak eyes. I had to put my chair up by the chalkboard and stand up to see the problems. It was not until years later when I was teaching, and had so many papers to grade of my own, that I realized all of my teachers had to grade my papers separately. They could not use an answer key since I would often copy the problem wrong but have the right answer for what I had written. I don't remember hearing even one of them complain. They did this for the first five and a half years.

In our small school, the superintendent would pick out a student to substitute teach if a teacher had to miss school. My sixth grade teacher was absent one day and my sister, Wanda, was asked to teach our class. When she saw that I was putting my chair up to the board and still having to stand up to see, she couldn't believe it. She went home and said, "Daddy, you've got to get Patsy some glasses. She can't see anything!" I finally got glasses and can still vividly remember seeing individual bricks in buildings and the individual leaves on the trees for the first time.

Mr. Fields, our superintendent was new to the school when I started in first grade. In addition to his administrative duties, he taught math, drove a school bus, and coached basketball and volleyball. His wife taught English, typing, Spanish, and book-keeping. Mr. Fields never hesitated to take off his belt and use it when he felt the children needed it. We were all afraid of him. If we heard a board creak in the old wooden floor of the hallway, we would get deathly quiet. Some children seemed to get the belt over and over.

Mr. Fields was a really good math teacher as to the subject matter, but greatly lacked in the area of compassion for students. He taught grades 7–12. He would send us to the board almost every day to work problems, so he could see if we understood how to do them. He and my sister, Helene, did not get along. She was captain of the girls' basketball team, and he was their coach. She was one of the very few in the school who was not afraid of him. She would cuss him out if he scolded her too much. She was so angry with him that she refused to learn math.

The first day of class in seventh grade math, Mr. Fields sent us to the chalkboard. He yelled at me, "Now, Patsy, keep your eyes on your own work! You're just like your sister, Helene!" It broke my heart to have him accuse me of cheating. The truth was that others were more apt to copy from me. I liked math and enjoyed working the problems as though they were puzzles to be solved. After a few days, he began to see that I was doing well and then started using me to substitute teach. On one occasion, he sent me to the freshman math class to teach. I went to the chalkboard and started showing them how to do the problems.

Helene, on the other hand, continued to refuse to do math because she was in a power struggle with Mr. Fields. After she graduated from high school, she got a job as bookkeeper for Mason Motor Company in Monett. Her husband, Gene, worked there as a mechanic. Being a bookkeeper required her to also greet people and take their money for services rendered. On Sundays, when she and Gene would come to dinner, she would motion for me to come with her. We would go in the back bedroom where she would take a big handful of change from her purse. She wanted me to teach her how to make change. We would sit for an hour or so practicing making change so she could do her job in Monett. She caught on fast and did very well in her job. A few years later, when she quit in order to give birth to her first child, the company had to hire two people to take her place!

It was interesting that the superintendent's family was Cherokee. Prejudice was still common in those days. I remember hearing my mom remark once when Mrs. Fields was walking down the street, "Look at her. She looks just like a nigger!" In fact, Verona, I found, had a law on the books that no black person was to neither set foot in the town nor let the sun go down on him/her. I learned this when I noticed a black man sitting in a delivery truck that had come to our grocery store from Springfield. I asked my mom why he didn't help unload the boxes and was told about the law that prevented him from setting a foot in our town. I felt so sad to hear this. That was the first black person I had ever seen, and I certainly didn't understand why there would be such a law. It is ironic that years later, when my husband and I were working on the Navajo reservation, we found that there had been a great deal of intermarriage between the black people and the Cherokee tribe. There was a good chance that the Fields family was part black, yet Mr. Fields was superintendent for probably more than twenty years and even became mayor of the town!

If it was the intent of the law to breed prejudice, it didn't work. Those of us who grew up there were never around black people and had no reason not to like them. To my knowledge, most of us grew up with no racial prejudice at all. The people who made that law had passed away, and the generation that raised us didn't seem to have the feelings of those before it.

When I was in third grade, Mr. Fields came to our class and announced that we had a new family who had moved to town and a new student for our class. A gentleman had returned to Verona from World War II with a Filipino bride and three children. Mr. Fields placed the new student, Nina Ham, in first grade, but she quickly moved up to third grade. She and I became good friends for most of the school years. We would study together and play together. She lived down the street from our grocery store, so we were within easy walking distance. Upon graduation, she went on to Drury College in Springfield to study to become a nurse.

The Great Depression and WWII impacted the classroom. I recall buying savings stamps for ten cents each and sticking them in a book to help pay for military equipment for our soldiers. The war started when I was in elementary school, so we heard quite a bit about it through our battery-operated radio and the newspapers. In our local effort to help our troops, we had scrap iron drives and contests to see which class could collect the most scrap iron that could be trucked away and melted down to make war equipment. The government distributed ration books that held stamps. One stamp could be used to buy a certain amount of sugar. Another stamp could be used to buy a certain amount of gas, etc. This was a way to be fair to families by allowing everyone to have a little of the hard-to-get items. Imported items were rare or impossible to obtain. There was no bubble gum because rubber came from another country. This meant that sugar and pineapple were very scarce as well because they had to come by ship. Daddy named one lady "Miss Pineapple" because she came to town every Saturday and went to all three grocery stores looking for sugar and pineapple. She was a hoarder and would try to get things for herself. "She probably has a basement full of that stuff!" people would say. My dad looked on this practice with disdain. He felt she and others like her should be more considerate. Other memories of how things were different then stuck in my mind. We had little red and green plastic tokens to use like money. Ten tokens equaled one penny. A penny was more valuable then. There was also a soup truck that came to town. I remember standing with my dad in front of the grocery store and seeing a red truck come to town and park by the post office. A man got out, opened the back of the truck, climbed up in the truck and started ladling soup from a large kettle into cups and bowls clutched in the hands of hungry people in line behind the truck. I didn't realize at the time how blessed our family was to have the farm and grocery store. We never had to use the soup line.

One of the most frightening experiences we had was the practice of blackout nights. We would be told via radio that on a certain night, we were to extinguish all lights. We would put out our kerosene lights and listen for planes to fly over the farmhouse. Sometimes, my sisters and I would hide under the beds. Our parents told us that this was a practice drill. In case the Japanese planes decided to bomb us, they couldn't see any lights to know where to drop the bombs. Many buildings had heavy black shades made for windows to keep the light from showing through.

On one occasion, we happened to drive past Camp Crowder in Neosho, Missouri, and saw war prisoners behind fences with guards. That was a troubling image for a young child to process in mind. Camp Crowder is now Crowder College, and pictures of the time when prisoners were kept there are on exhibit at the college.

Finally, one morning, the announcement was made on our battery radio that the Japanese had surrendered. I was nine years old at the time. I ran as hard as I could to the barn to tell my dad that the war had ended. We were all so very relieved!

Immediately following the war, we started looking forward to our troops coming home. When my uncle returned, we learned he had lost one eye. A cousin had spent time in a prison camp in Japan. When they came home, we were overjoyed. I vividly remember the Sunday afternoon when my cousin and his family came to see us. He told us how much weight he had lost in prison where rice was the common food. He also counted one to ten for us in Japanese! Rosemary and I went to school the next week bragging about how we could say nine and ten in Japanese.

Many of the military brought home some souvenirs. One popular souvenir was Japanese silk. It was bright orange, and, as I recall, we were told that it was used for the Japanese parachutes. Many of the ladies made dresses or blouses of it and proudly wore them for the next few years. I remember going to the Pentecostal church in Monett with my dad and seeing one of the teen girls wearing her see-through Japanese silk blouse. It was acceptable at church because the Pentecostals believed in wearing long sleeves. I failed to understand the reasoning that would allow a see-through blouse but forbid short sleeves!

When the war ended, we could get bubble gum, pineapple, and the other things that had been rationed. There was lots of talk about the atomic bomb. One cereal box came out with a coupon for an atomic bomb ring. Some of my girlfriends and I decided to order those rings and form an atomic bomb club. They were perfect! They had a metal capsule on top that would open up. We would make up secret codes, write messages, and put the messages inside the rings.

Next to the home of one of my friends was a vacant lot, about a block from the school, which had an old abandoned concrete cellar. I'm sure it had served its duty well at one time to store canned goods and garden produce when a house stood next to it. This time, it would serve again in a different capacity as a clubhouse for my girlfriends and me. We would meet after school in our clubhouse and put up pictures of the movie stars we liked most. Rita Hayworth, Lana Turner, Cornel Wilde, Rock Hudson, and others graced the walls of the old cellar. Not to be outdone, some of the boys formed a black axe club. They chose an old barn next to the same vacant lot as a clubhouse. We would be chatting when suddenly small rocks would fall down through the little vent on top of the cellar. The boys were sneaking up on us to see if they could hear what we were saying. Then, the chase would begin! We would come out of the cellar and start chasing the boys. They would run to their hideout and go up into the loft. Then, we would sneak up on them to see if we could hear what they were saying. This scenario was repeated innumerable times. Sometimes, we would catch the guys by the tails of their shirts and slug it out. We kept their moms busy sewing buttons back on their shirts!

One of our favorite games was keep-away. When we weren't doing the club activities, we played this made-up game on the school playground. Rules were simple. Girls kept the ball away from the boys. Boys tried to keep the ball away from the girls. There were no boundaries. It was a pretty rough game, but we loved it and played it many afternoons while waiting for the late school bus or for my folks to close the grocery store and go home to the farm.

⚜

Things were different then. Mom would lay a garment on the floor on some newspaper and cut out a pattern to make a new garment. Chicken feed came in printed cloth sacks. She used these sacks to make dresses for my sisters and me. We carried in wood for the wood stove in the winter with socks on our hands since we didn't have gloves. Regardless of the weather, we walked to the end of the gravel lane to catch the school bus. Sometimes, it was very cold. One morning, when I got to school, Miss Mary had me sit by the radiator, got a bucket of water, and placed my feet in it because she thought they might be frozen.

When Christmas came each year, we would walk out in the woods and cut a cedar tree and decorate it with anything we could. We made paper chains of construction paper to put on it. We didn't string popcorn. We probably thought it was more important to eat it! I saved green stamps to get $2.50 each Christmas for shopping. They were given by some of the merchants when purchases were made. They could be redeemed for merchandise or cash. One book of green stamps could be redeemed for $2.50. My sisters laughed for years about the Blue Waltz perfume I bought for each of them for ten cents a bottle.

A great amount of attention was paid each year to the school and church Christmas programs. There were many rehearsals of the parts assigned to those who were in the programs. Everyone worried about looking their very best. Shoes were polished, dresses were starched and ironed, and hair was shampooed and curled. Everyone looked forward to receiving the sack of candy containing an orange and apple from the church. We had very little fruit during the winter, and nothing tasted quite as sweet as those big navel oranges. There was always a chocolate or two in each sack as well.

On one particular Christmas, Mom and Dad bought me a light-chocolate-colored blouse with a black bow tie and white collar and cuffs to go with a new dark green skirt. I was eager to go back to school to wear it. On that first day back to school, I got dressed in the back bedroom as I usually did and went to the living room to stand by the wood stove to keep warm until the bus came. "Here comes the bus!" my sister yelled. We grabbed our coats and ran out the door. As soon as I stepped out the door, my skirt burst into flames. My sisters grabbed the bucket of water we used for drinking (we didn't have running water at the time) and doused me! I felt them beating me with brooms and yelling at me. I lay down on the ground and rolled over. We got the fire out just as the bus, with all the kids on it, drove into the yard! Though sad and embarrassed, I dragged myself back in to the house. The bus went on without me and after I changed, my mom took me to school I sure hated to lose that pretty green skirt but we managed to save the blouse.

Mom would save her eggs and take them to town on Saturdays to sell and get money to buy something that was needed. She always emphasized the importance of dressing properly and looking neat and clean when we went anywhere away from home. In my case, I had to sit and have someone, usually Ernestine, use a curling iron on my hair. I was the only one with straight hair. My four sisters had dark brown hair with some natural curl. My hair was blonde and very, very, straight. I can still hear and see in my mind the image of my mom looking down at me and saying, "Patsy, what in the world are we going to do with that hair?" On this occasion, as usual, mom had us all dressed up in starched and ironed homemade dresses, and clean, polished shoes. While we were in Penney's, a lady came up and started talking to my mom. "Ethel", she said, "I don't know how you do it. You always have all of your daughters looking so nice! They are all so pretty!" We were all feeling good and probably beaming with pride. She and my mom talked for a little while and when she got ready to leave, she looked down at me and said, "Now, Ethel, is this one yours, too? She doesn't look like the rest of them!" For the remainder of my youthful years, I always felt like the ugly duckling from the story by the same name. What a valuable lesson to remind me today that children are listening, too.

Strawberry season was a special time in Verona! Every spring, right after school was out, usually the third week of May, my sisters and I each got a new straw hat to get ready to pick berries. Those who planned to pick would meet at our store building in the morning, load up in the old red truck, and head for the berry field on the forty acres my dad had bought. The pickers got seven cents for each quart picked, except for my sisters and I who got only five cents for each quart. My dad felt that since we were family, we shouldn't get paid as much. Picking berries was hard! The stems had to be left about one inch long. We had to squat and waddle along the rows. We didn't dare step on a berry or miss any. That would be wasteful. I can remember my hands being swollen so that I could barely see my knuckles. We would sweat so much that there would be wet spots on our clothing. Our carriers would hold six quarts and we had to mound them up. Then, we would carefully carry them to the berry shed where my mom and other ladies were culling the berries. Only the good ones were crated and taken in the truck to Monett to be shipped out by train. The culls went home with us, and we had to help mom stem and wash them to be canned that night for food for the next winter.

Monett was known in those days as the strawberry capital of the world. At this time of year, hobos would arrive on the train that ran through Verona. The hobos knew they could find work there picking strawberries. One hobo, Old Blue Nose, would arrive every spring. He really did have a big bluish nose. He was a good berry picker. He found a place to live in a shed behind someone's house. Other hobos camped out on the river during the season, and we were not allowed to go down to the river during that time. When the picking season was over, daddy would start new patches of berries. Some of my sisters and I had to help separate and plant the new startings so there would be a berry patch for the next year.

During one berry season, my dad had trouble with his knee. It went out of place, and he went to the two-story white building in town to see Doc Watson. The doctor gave my dad some morphine and pulled and tugged on his leg to get it to go back in place. My dad hobbled around all during berry season. I helped milk the twenty-five cows we owned and slopped the hogs. My mom could really milk cows! We had an old milking machine that would milk one cow at a time. I would put it on one cow and sit down and milk another cow while the machine was doing its job. At the same time, my mom would milk two cows by hand! Daddy had built a milk house of field rock. He had vats of water in it with large cream cans. I would take my bucket and the milking machine to the milk house and pour the milk through a strainer into the cans. I'm not sure how long we did this before my dad's knee got better.

It was not until I was grown and my knee went out of place that I realized what had happened to my dad. My first experience of this happened when I stooped down to look at some pottery at the Hopi villages in Arizona. When I started to get up, I couldn't straighten out my leg. I broke out in a sweat and got really weak. I reached down behind my knee and began to massage it. As I leaned on my husband, I continued to massage it and finally saw my knee cap move back in place. The pain stopped. I suspect that my dad had the same problem. My niece later told me that it was caused by not having strong enough ligaments and muscles to hold it in place. At any rate, whatever the cause, it was not easy for our family when my dad fell out of the berry patch as my brothers-in-law laughingly accused him of doing. They had always laughed about how steep the hills were on the second farm he bought.

It became more and more difficult to find pickers. By the time I was in high school, berries were no longer grown around Verona. Most strawberries began coming from California. However, those berry-pickin' days had lots of stories.

∾

There were many people having trouble making ends meet in my younger days. Often, people would come to the farmhouse wanting work and something to eat. There is an image in my mind of a man sitting on the step with a plate of food in his hand that my mom had fixed for him. It seems that somehow, some way, my mom could always make a plate of food for anyone who came to our door. Mom seemed to like raising chickens. Every spring, a box of chickens would come to the post office and those little fluffy balls would be peeping as we went to get them. Daddy would help her fix a place to care for them, and she would raise some to be layers and others to be eaten. During the night, if daddy heard a ruckus in the chicken house, he would grab his shotgun and head that way. Some people were so hungry they were stealing those that were big enough to eat for food. My folks would not allow stealing, but if anyone came and asked for help, I don't remember them ever turning anyone away. Usually, the people in need didn't expect to just eat a meal without doing some work for it. There was always work to be done around the farm.

There was a group of gypsies who came to Verona almost every summer. They had covered wagons. Sometimes, they would camp between Verona and Monett beside the highway. People were leery of them. There were rumors that they could not be trusted and that they would steal. Everyone watched their chickens especially well when they were around.

As children, we loved to explore. We explored caves, abandoned houses, or walked along the river to see what we could find. One place we explored was the ruins of the old building that had served as the first Sunday school west of the Mississippi River and south of the Missouri River. There was a small cave near it, and we spent many hours playing there. It was just past the old red mill that stood as a testimony of the tough days of the past.

Although the old mill was no longer used to make flour, it served as a source of entertainment to those of us who liked to explore it. It was in the grassy field adjacent to it that our class would often have its end of school picnic. We would hike there from school as a group. First, we would put our pop bottles in the edge of the river to cool them down; then, we would play red rover, dodgeball, or work-up softball until lunch. At that time, we would pull our pop from the edge of the river, get our sack lunches, and enjoy our meal.

High school was not quite as pleasurable as elementary school, but it still held its exciting events. The junior class always put on one play each year and the senior class did two plays. It was always a big thing to find out who got the leading roles. Much time was spent on these plays. Students worked and worked to memorize their parts. We did not have proms. Our community did not believe in dancing. Instead, we had banquets for the juniors and seniors. All the girls looked forward to getting a new formal for the banquets. Everyone was using good manners, and we always had a guest speaker to extol the virtues of pious living. Many a girl had her first date for the banquets. That was the case with me. Since our class was so small, there were really not a lot of guys to pick from. It was not until I went to college that I really started dating. I had only three or four dates in high school. Actually, it was surprising that I had that many because there was a rumor around town that you'd better not date those Haddock girls. Old man Haddock was said to have a shotgun. This weeded out the faint of heart! Those brave enough to take the chance always went through the grueling experience of meeting my dad and answering questions. My dad had a way of summing up a guy, and they went away with complete understanding that they had better take care of his girls!

From the time I started first grade, I had dreamed of being valedictorian of my graduating class. At the end of my junior year, I had enough credits to graduate, but the state legislature passed a law that everyone had to take a one-fourth credit of Missouri Constitution. I thought that I might as well take a full load since I had to go back to school anyway. I graduated with more credits than I needed and was awarded a scholarship to Southwest Missouri State Teacher's College in Springfield.

I knew in my heart that I had to go to college although none of my sisters had done so. I went to Springfield to find a job. I refused to lie and say that I planned to stay on the job past summer. The only job I could get was working at a variety store. At the same time, I worked as a cook, babysitter, and housekeeper for a teacher. She was single with one school-age son. She had attended School of the Ozarks before it became a college and had worked her way through high school. Perhaps I imagined it, but it seemed that she was bitter about her experience and was trying to get revenge by taking it out on those who worked for her. I did not enjoy working for her.

I thought I would really like to work at the variety store because they assigned me to work in the fabric department. I had always liked to sew and I loved fabrics. There were two older ladies who worked there. They seemed sweet enough, but somewhat reserved. I was naïve and trusted them too much. One day, the manager told me that he was going to let me go. I pressed him as to the reason. First, he told me that business was down due to the drought. I continued to press him until he told me that some money had been missing from the cash register. I told him that I was a Christian and did not do that kind of thing. It took me some time to realize that probably one or both of the ladies was taking the money and blaming it on me. I was devastated!

My Aunt Opie was living in Springfield, and she wanted me to live with her. I moved in with her, but things just didn't seem right. One night, I looked out the window at the stars and told God how confused I was. "God," I said, "I don't even know if you still hear me, but I need help. Please show me what to do!" The next weekend, I went home to Verona and stopped by the house of my senior class sponsor. I asked her if she had ever gotten the results of the Ohio Psychological Test that the seniors had taken. I was mostly asking out of pride just to see how I did. She said she would check and let me know.

I went home again the next weekend to find my family all excited. My class sponsor had put a news release in the local papers that I had made the highest score on the Ohio Psychological Test ever recorded in Lawrence County, and that I was awarded a scholarship to Missouri University and would be working in the office of Dean Townsend in the school of education! I had not even told her that I wanted to go there. After it had been put in the paper, there was no way that I was going to back out. My pride would not let me do that. What would people think? This was all the Lord's doing. I remember taking that test and looking at all the big words I had never heard, and praying and asking God to help me check the right answers. I still remember the word "philanthropist" and wondered what in the world that meant! At any rate, I began to make plans to go to Missouri University in the fall. My aunt was not happy with me. She said, "You'll never make it up there. You have to be rich and belong to a sorority before you can make it there!" Now, I realize that she just wanted me to stay with her. At the time, it really hurt. I had a sense of rightness about this, and I was determined to try my best.

As she talked, I thought of the $125 I had managed to save during the summer. The scholarship paid only $125 for two semesters. Somehow, though, there was still that sense of rightness about it.

When my former youth pastor from the little Methodist church in Verona heard about my scholarship, he offered to mortgage his farm to get money for me to go on to college. I will never forget that! My folks were discouraging me and said they could not afford to help me at all, and yet he was willing to mortgage his farm. Of course, I refused. There was no way I wanted that heavy load on me. I felt that if God wanted me to go, he would provide.

It was necessary to make a trip to Columbia to register and talk to someone about financial aid. My dad drove me to Springfield in the old red truck to catch the bus. "Now, Patsy," he said, "I don't know why you can't be like the other girls. They all got married and are raising a family. Why can't you do that?" I tried the best way I knew to tell him that I felt like I had to go to college. He told me that he had always been hard on me because he was afraid I would let it go to my head when I succeeded at anything. When he mentioned that he had always been hard on me, images flashed in my mind of the many times I had worked so hard to win his approval by taking home a good report card. At those times he would often say, "Well, Patsy, I don't know what to say except just remember that you don't learn everything in books. Just look at that guy that runs around Verona, so crazy. Why, he went to some of those fancy colleges back East and he's nothing more than an 'ejecated' fool." That's about all I remember from the conversation.

When the bus crossed the Missouri river in Jefferson City, I thought that Daniel Boone probably was not as afraid when he came that way as I was. I had never been this far away from home before. I had no idea what to do except to go to Jesse Hall and talk to the financial advisor. When I got there, I got off the bus praying that the Lord would show me where to go. I walked straight to Jesse Hall. I kept thinking of the Bible verse, "You shall know the truth and the truth shall set you free." I talked to the financial aid person and was told that all freshmen were required to live in the dorm. I knew I could not afford that. She finally gave me the names and addresses of some off-campus houses that I could contact. She said that my name would be put on a list of babysitters, so that when people called, I would be referred to them. I never knew where my sponsor had gotten the idea of me working in the dean's office. The financial aid office did, however, find me a job in the education reading room of the library.

The Tiger Tower stood above the other buildings, so I figured I could find it. I got a room there for the night. I decided to walk a little bit and see what I could see. I got lost and was wondering around. It got dark, and I was really frightened. A car drove up beside me and a guy tried to pick me up. I just kept walking and would not talk. Finally, he said, "What are you, anyway, a school teacher?" It was easy to tell that he did not like school teachers. I finally found my way back to the hotel. I caught the bus home the next day.

I wrote to the places I had been given for off-campus housing. I got a letter back from Nora Black, who owned a house with her sister, Lottie, across the street from the education building. The only room she had left was the least expensive in the house. It was on third floor and my roommate would be a Mennonite girl. Cooking privileges were in the basement. We each had a shelf to store our groceries and there were two refrigerators for us to use. I can't remember for sure, but I think there were around twenty girls who stayed in the house. What an answer to prayer! God was truly working. I stayed in this house all four years of college. One time, Miss Nora and I were chatting, and she told me how careful she was about the girls she let to stay in the house. "I always talk to the girls face to face," she said. "I never take anyone just from a letter!" I said, "Miss Nora, you took me from just my letter." "Yours was different," she said. "It just sounded right." Another sign that God had been working!

My sister Ernestine started sewing me some feedsack sheets. She used four white feedsacks and sewed them together with flat fell seams. I didn't mind having to sleep on the rough seam. I just appreciated her doing it for me. Helene was canning and got some canned goods together for me to take. I had one old blue suitcase to take and the other things were put in cardboard boxes. I was ready for college!

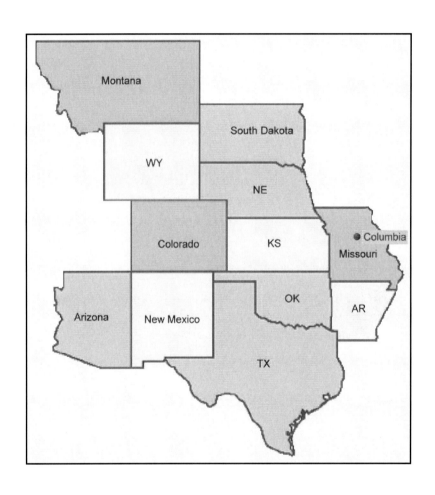

Off to College

Columbia, MO

*D*addy had sold some cattle and bought a brand new '54 Chevy not too long before the time for me to go off to college. Daddy never bought anything he couldn't pay cash for. Daddy and Mom; Ernestine and her husband, Whitie; and my younger sister Rosemary; and me all piled into the new car and headed to Columbia with my blue suitcase and two or three cardboard boxes in the trunk. Rosemary says that she still remembers stopping in front of the big three-story white house and helping unload my few belongings, setting them on the sidewalk, and then driving away leaving me standing there looking scared and forlorn. I suspect my dad was in a hurry to get home before dark or perhaps concerned about work awaiting him there. Looking back now, it seems strange that they didn't come in and see where I would be staying.

I carried my few things inside. Miss Nora welcomed me with a smile and showed me the basement and my room. I began to unpack my few things. I was totally pleased with my sweet roommate. She was in the Marching Mizzou band and was majoring in music. Every night, she read her Bible before going to bed. Again, God had worked to put me with the right person in the right place. We got along with each other very well. She was very quiet, so we each could study. It was a small room. Each half of the room had a twin-size bed, a dresser, a desk, and a place to hang clothes.

I chose to major in home economics mainly because that was the thing I thought I needed the most. Mom had not been big on teaching us how to do homemaking. Besides, I had helped daddy outside most of the time. Mom didn't like for us to make messes in the kitchen. Ernestine, on the other hand, was mom's helper in the kitchen. The rest of us were sort of on our own. I had always wanted to teach school and felt the importance of family life. I knew that what I learned in home economics would help me the rest of my life.

I passed all of my entrance exams. I missed getting into the higher English class by one point. This turned out to be a good thing. Those who were placed in that class had a lot more work expected of them. Some of those placed in remedial class ended up in a class with a professor who felt that anyone in that class was below average; therefore, he never gave a grade of average or above.

All of my freshman classes were on the third floor of some building. We had ten minutes to get from one class to another. There was lots of walking! Sometimes, I would have to go from the white campus to the red campus between classes. It was a big place for a girl from the small town of Verona.

I never understood why some of the classes for majoring in home economics were required. I was required to take two chemistry classes. Most of the time, in the inorganic chemistry class, we studied about how to extract bromine from seawater. In the organic chemistry class, we made perfumes. A food chemistry class or a class about chemicals in soaps would have been much more helpful.

The inorganic chemistry class was located in a large auditorium where more than a hundred students fearfully awaited meeting the professor. He was dean of the school for chemistry and had written the textbook that was about a half-inch thick.

He had just hit the high spots and really did not explain anything in the book. His lectures were similar. He lectured as though he was commenting on things we already knew. On the first day of class, he told us to look at the person on the right. "Now look at the person on your left," he said. "If statistics are true and if history truly does repeat itself, then that person on your right or your left or you will fail this course. In the past, one-third of the students have failed this course." What a way to instill confidence in students! Verona High School had not offered chemistry. I hardly knew what a Bunsen burner was or had never handled a test tube. I found that many of the students in the class were premed students from St. Louis and Kansas City. They had all taken chemistry in their high schools. I was scared!

By the middle of the semester, I had a low I (inferior) grade. At that time, the grades were E, S, M, I, and F, for excellent, superior, mediocre, inferior, and failure. I knew I was in trouble. I attended the discussion groups for help. There, I found a leader of the group who was a foreign student who spoke with such a dialect that I could not understand. Further, he discussed different topics than those being covered in the lecture. The lecture was about one thing, the lab was about another, and the discussion group about still another topic in chemistry. My mind was getting more and more confused. I prayed and prayed about this class. I simply could not understand the text. Finally, it was the end of the semester. The dean announced that the final exam was written for a three-hour exam. "Of course," he said, "I cannot require you to attend for three hours because the university has set up this course for a two-hour exam. However, I will be here at 7 a.m. for those of you who want to come at that time."

After much prayer, I decided that I was going to learn something in that class whether I passed it or not. I remembered the high school chemistry books in the back room of our education reading room in the library where I worked. I checked out three or four of them and took them to my room. I stayed in my room all weekend except for going to church. I started reading at the front of the dean's textbook, and each time there was something I didn't understand, I looked it up in one of the high school textbooks. I managed to get about half way through the book over the weekend.

The exam had been scheduled for 7 a.m. on Monday morning. It was January, and the temperature was below zero. It was dark as I trudged across to the white campus. As I think about it, I can still remember the chill I felt in my shin bones. (We still wore dresses most of the time in the '50s.) I was so frightened, but I had the satisfaction of knowing that I had learned some things and had put in a good effort over the weekend. I was fairly calm as I took the exam, full knowing that I was apt to fail the course. It was a few days before the grades were posted. Finally, we all crowded around the bulletin board to check our grades. I had made an M for the course!

Trips home were few and far between. Sometimes, I could catch a ride with someone going that way, but often, my family gave me a hard time while I was there. I kept hearing, "Don't think you're smarter than us just because you are going to college!" On one such occasion, my dad was talking to me like that, and I was close to tears. As he walked out the door, he stopped and listened to the news. He turned to me and said, "That's what I woulda been if I could've got an ejecation. I'd a been a politician!" In later years, I realized that my dad was hurting because he could not do what I was doing. I dare to think he might actually have been a little jealous.

Early during the first semester, a girl in our house, Doris McDowell, invited me to go to the Baptist Student Center with her. That was the beginning of a special friendship for me. It was also the beginning of many wonderful experiences with Christian students. I became active in the happenings at the center and active at Memorial Baptist Church. The student center had vespers every evening and I hardly ever missed. My college life revolved around babysitting, working at the library, studying, and the BSU (Baptist Student Union). Actually, it was an ideal situation.

There were two ordained ministers in charge at the Baptist Student Center. One of them taught Bible classes where college students could take Bible courses for credits. The other was a student pastor who was very kind and very, very energetic. He used to say, "I'd rather wear out than rust out!" The friend who invited me was the secretary. She was a very unique person!

Doris was always laughing! She was a ray of sunshine and reflected God's love wherever she happened to be. She was not shy about telling others about Christ. If we were having a party, she would ask perfect strangers to come. She was a year or two older than me and seemed to have all the answers. She was just what I needed. Looking back, however, I have to wonder if the feeling was mutual. I may have burdened her with my needs. We were together most of the time when it was possible. She invited me to Memorial Baptist Church where I attended during all four years of school. Not very many students had cars. Those students who did have cars were imposed upon by the rest of us to get to church or other activities. She knew how to make the arrangements and keep things moving in the right direction.

My experiences working in various activities at the Baptist Student Center and Memorial Baptist Church were the highlights in my life. I had various responsibilities at various times. On one occasion, it was my responsibility to be on hand to welcome people to the center who happened to drop in. A couple of guys came in, and I began chatting with them. During the conversation, one of them asked me what I was majoring in. When I hesitated, he said, "I know what you are! You're a teacher!" He said it with the same tone and inflection I had heard on my first night in Columbia when the fellow tried to pick me up. My heart jumped up in my throat, and I had to work hard to control my feelings. As it turned out, some time later, he asked me out, and I accepted making sure there were others present at all times until I knew everything was safe. He started going to church with some of us, and some weeks later, he phoned me to tell me that he was walking out to the church and praying. He said that he had been saved on the way to the church.

There were several young ministers who were active at the Baptist Student Center. We would have teams go out to neighboring communities to work in some of the churches. One young minister, Tommy Hill, asked me if I would go with him to Portland on Sundays to play the piano for him. Tommy was an energetic young fellow and radiated enthusiasm for letting others know about Jesus. We would leave on Sunday morning, he would preach at the church, and I would play the piano. A family from the church always took us home with them for lunch. In the afternoons, we would go door to door to invite people to the church. Then, we would go back for our second meal of pancakes at their home and repeat in the evening the routine of the morning service.

Portland was an interesting little town by the Missouri River. Most of the houses were two-story old homes that were partly rotted. The moisture from the river had taken its toll on all the structures. We would walk up on the porches and it seemed as though the whole house would shake. Most houses were occupied on the lower floor only to save on heating fuel. There was usually a rag stuffed along the bottom of the door to keep out the cold air.

On one occasion, Tommy and I walked up on a porch, knocked on the door and heard a gruff voice from inside say, "Who is it?" We answered that we were from the Baptist church. "Nope, don't want nuthin' to do with it!" he said. After telling him that we just wanted to get to know him, we went on our way. We didn't forget him, though. We kept going back there each Sunday. Eventually, he let us in and we visited with him by his old wood stove. Little by little, he grew to like us, and we considered him a real fascination. We heard some time after we quit going to Portland that he had finally accepted Christ.

Doris and I tried to attend everything at church that we possibly could. I watched many of the students go forward and say that God had called them to missions or full-time Christian service. I was puzzled. When I accepted Christ as a small child, I had told God that I would be a missionary if he wanted me to do so. Did he not want me? Was I not as good as the others? Why was he calling them and not me? I prayed a great deal about this.

One evening, Doris and I went to Memorial Baptist Church to a revival service. We were laughing and giggling and having fun. We were not even thinking serious thoughts that night. I didn't pay real close attention to the sermon, but when the invitation was given, I had a strange feeling that I was supposed to go forward. I was again puzzled. I kept feeling an urging, but didn't want to do something that I wasn't sure about. I prayed and asked God what I was to do. I said in my mind that if the next song they sang was "Wherever He Leads I'll Go," then I would go forward. Sure enough, that was the next song announced. Still, I wanted to be sure, and I held back. I couldn't believe it, but my legs just started moving. I had a burning sensation in my legs up to my knees and my heart was pounding. My legs were just carrying me up to the front of the church! When I got there, I told the preacher that I was being called for full-time Christian service.

At this writing, I count sixteen houses and six different states where I have lived.

Doris babysat for a doctor who practiced in Columbia. Some of their friends needed a babysitter. I began babysitting for their friends. I'm not sure I would have made it without this wonderful family. Dr. and Mrs. Ladenson (Roland and Ginny) had three children. He practiced medicine in Columbia and donated time to teach a class in heart disease at the university. I was told many times that I was just like one of the family to them. I loved those children....and still do! The oldest son, Paul, is now a doctor at a prestigious hospital in the East. The second son, Reid, honored us by coming to see us when we lived in Albuquerque in later years. I am still in communication with the daughter, Ann, who is the youngest.

My college family lived a few blocks from where I lived, and some of the time, I could walk to their home. Most of the time, however, Ginny would call a cab to come and pick me up. I thought their house was beautiful. It was fancier than any I had ever seen. I was in awe whenever Dr. Ladenson came around. In those days, doctors were almost revered. I always felt he was so smart that I was intimidated by him. His wife, however, had a wonderful way of putting everyone at ease. She was one of those rare people whose presence motivated you to want to achieve more. She was so diplomatic! She always seemed to know the right thing to say at the right time. She was small of frame, and I always thought of her as a jenny wren because she was always flitting around getting things done. I would always try to clean up any mess the children or I made, but I would not wash the liquor glasses and would not lie on the phone to say that the doctor was not available. He wasn't real happy with me about that. He teased me about not washing the glasses, but I didn't want to touch them.

I liked to tell the children Bible stories, and they seemed to like to hear them. I would tuck them in at night and hear their prayers. After they were in bed, I would try to study. On one occasion, while trying to study, I had the TV on and Elvis Presley came on. I thought he was vulgar, so I turned off the set. He was very popular with a lot of the college students. In fact, one Sunday evening after church, some of us went to Howard Johnson's for ice cream. He was sitting with the girl he was dating from Stephen's College in his pink Cadillac. Even though I was unimpressed, the others were excited about seeing him.

Ann, the daughter, was allergic to eggs, so we always had to watch that she didn't get anything with eggs as an ingredient. A lady from the community worked for the family during the day to clean and care for the youngest children in case the parents were gone. On one occasion, the parents went to Denver to a medical conference. I stayed in the home at night, and the other lady stayed there during the day while I was in classes. One night, while they were gone, Ann got sick and was just limp in my arms. I immediately called the pediatrician, and he came and cared for her. That was quite scary. To this day, I don't know what she had with eggs, or whether it was I or the other lady who let her have it. At any rate, she was fine by the time the parents got back home.

Columbia seemed to have many storms. On one occasion, while I was with the children, we had a really bad one. I called the children together and asked Paul to find candles for us. As Ann was coming downstairs, she said, "Patsy, my stomach hurts!" I think she was frightened and didn't know what else to say. We all huddled in the corner of the kitchen where we thought we would be away from where a tree might fall on the house. Lots of limbs blew down, but no windows broke, and we weathered the storm just fine. When the parents came home, they laughed about having dinner in a new home that had windows all across one side of it. They got to see a big picture of the storm with all of its lightning and trees blowing! I'm not sure those folks were so glad they had put in all of the windows they had!

When I was a senior, I got sick with Asian flu. Ginny came, fetched me from where I was staying, and took me to their home. They had a guest room on the third floor, and that became my room for a week or so. Every afternoon, Roland would come upstairs, and check me after he came home from his office. I was worried because it was almost time for me to go to Hannibal to do my student teaching. Home economics education majors were required to spend time off-campus observing in a high school setting and then actually taking over the class. A few days before I was scheduled to go, Roland told me it was time for me to get out of bed and get my strength back. I did so. I was downstairs in the kitchen when Roland came home for lunch. He picked up the newspaper and commented about the trouble going on in Little Rock, Arkansas, where they were trying to integrate black people into the public schools. As we were discussing the racial tension, I mentioned that our church always counseled people when they went forward before they joined. He took offense at this. He said,

"You mean if I wanted to join your church, they wouldn't let me until they counseled me?" I tried to explain that the church simply wanted to be sure that people understood about salvation and were sincere in their decision. He went on to tell me that he was an atheist and didn't like churches and religion. I asked him how he thought the world was created, and he said that he thought there was a big ball spinning out in space and it evolved to become earth. My voice may have trembled with fear and respect for him as I told him how I believed. I also mentioned that I thought he was too smart to believe that. "Surely," I said, "you have seen people who you thought were ready to die, yet they kept on living. Doctors can't make a baby take its first breath. Only God can do that. There is only so much that men can do."

About that time, Ginny came home from where she had been, and the conversation stopped. That night, they went out to dinner, and I was to take care of the children. Ginny was all ready and sitting at the table tapping her fingers. Roland had gone outside, and she was waiting for him. I noticed that he looked at me a little strangely when he came in. The next day, I got ready to go to class. Ginny handed me a check. It was for much more than the babysitting the night before. "I can't take this," I said. "I owe you money for taking care of me. You don't owe me money!" "Roland said you would say that," Ginny said, "and he said to tell you that he is thankful for all God has done for him and wants to pass a little of it on to someone else!" I was overwhelmed.

I financed my student teaching with the check from Roland and Ginny and from the scholarship money I had won. At the end of my junior year, I happened to see a notice on the bulletin board at the house where I stayed about the Sarah Gentry Elston Scholarship. Not thinking that I had a ghost of a chance, I went ahead and applied for it. It was awarded to two outstanding women students by the Association of Women Students. I was selected as one of those students. This was a scholarship for $500 for each semester of my senior year. In addition, my dad had decided to give me a checkbook to use only for food. I guess he decided by now that I might make it after all! The fact that my being chosen for the scholarship was announced on KWTO radio station in spot announcements one day, probably helped as well. Also, I was called into the financial aid office one day and told that an anonymous donor had written a check for me for $25. It was suggested that I use it to buy an outfit to wear to church. To this day, I don't know who gave the check. I wrote a thank you note, and the financial aid person saw that the donor received it.

My student advisor had made arrangements for a place for me to stay in Hannibal. I had a room in a house with an older lady. There was a single guy renting a room from her also, and we had to share a bathroom. I was really uncomfortable, especially when the older lady decided she wanted to be a matchmaker. She always had a little half smile when we were both at the house at the same time. To make matters worse, I had an abscessed tooth while staying there. Since I had no car, he took me to the dentist. He waited for me and took me back to my room with my mouth full of bloody gauze! Needless to say, nothing ever came of her efforts to put us together!

My college days were coming to an end and a decision needed to be made as to what I was to do next. I never felt an inclination to go to seminary. My advisor called me in and discussed some openings for home economics teachers in Missouri. Nothing seemed to click. I went to the education building and checked the bulletin board there. One notice stuck out. A home economics teacher was needed in Sanders, Arizona. I checked maps and found that Sanders is located on the edge of the Navajo Indian Reservation. I couldn't get this place out of my mind. Besides, the job paid $4,400 per year, and home economics teaching jobs in Missouri were paying $3,600 or $3,800 per year. Doris had accepted a teaching job in California, and I was feeling adventurous too. This was too good to be true. I could do mission work with the Navajo people and get paid for it at the same time! I applied for the job and was accepted.

Our graduation was held in the football stadium. That was the first time I had been inside it. My mom and two of my sisters came to the graduation. My dad had not gone to my high school graduation and did not choose to come to my college graduation. I felt sad that he didn't come, but I was glad to see my mom and two sisters. Wanda was pregnant at the time. Little did I know then that someday, that little baby in her tummy would be playing football for Mizzou, and seeing him play there would be my first Mizzou football game to attend.

My mom took my diploma home and hung it on the wall and kept it there for years.

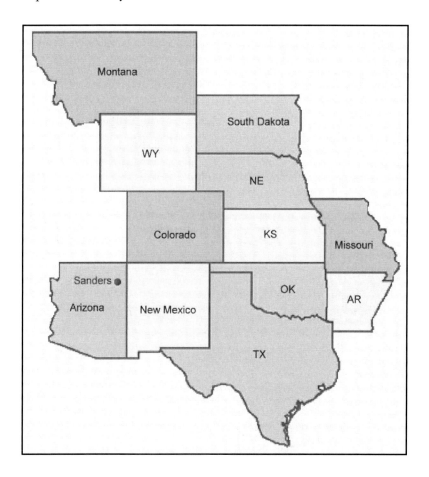

Here I am, Lord; I Trust You to Take Care of Me!

Sanders, Arizona

Upon graduation, I took my small savings to Mason Motor Company in Monett where my sister and brother-in-law worked. Mr. Mason was very kind to me and helped me pick out a car that had been used at a nearby high school as a driver's education car. It was a Fairlane 500 '57 Ford with four doors. It was beautiful! It was blue and white and had only four thousand miles on it. Payment arrangements were made, and the car was mine to drive home! It proved to be a good car in the years to come and got a great deal of use!

I can only imagine how my parents must have felt when I started out alone that August at age twenty. In 1958, there were still many misconceptions about the Indian people. Folks imagined that all Indians wore feathers and were like those seen in Western movies. In fact, my nephew had asked his mom if Indian children got a new feather grown in their head for each year of life! I knew absolutely no one in Arizona and had traveled very little in my life. My oldest sister, Ernestine, had made me some more sheets from her white cloth chicken feed sacks. They consisted of four sacks sewn together in flat-fell seams (the kind of seams used on the side of many jeans). My sisters, Helene and Wanda, gave me some home-canned food to take along. I was so excited that I probably overlooked any expressions of concern on their faces.

I started early in the morning and drove as far as Tucumcari, New Mexico, the first day. I stopped at the Sonic Drive-In and ordered a hamburger and then went across the street and rented a motel room. The next day, I drove through Albuquerque, Grants, and on through Gallup. On one occasion, when I stopped for gas, I was told that my fan belt was about to break. The service station attendant even showed me a tear in it. I bought a new one, he put it on, and I was on my way. Scams on Route 66 were common, and I have to wonder if he cut the belt. In the fifties, service station attendants would pump gas, clean windshields, and check under the hood. I understand that many fan belts were sold. From what I was later told, sometimes air would be let out of tires or the tires would actually be punctured and the innocent tourists would buy new tires.

I finally reached Gallup, New Mexico. Forty miles west of Gallup is the state line. Located at the state line of New Mexico and Arizona was an inspection station, post office, trading post, and school with small buildings nearby. That was Sanders. Arizona did not allow fruit to be brought into the state, so travelers were required to stop there and get rid of any fruit or plants they were carrying. I remember, as I came to Sanders, seeing several people standing by the inspection station eating fruit. Later, I learned that they were eating it so they wouldn't have to throw it away.

The school was not difficult to find. I went to the office and reported for work. The superintendent directed me to the teachers' quarters that were available for rent. The apartments were made of ammunition boxes left over from World War II. I made arrangements to rent one, and it didn't take long to move in with all of my few belongings. I had very few clothes, one cup, one fork, one spoon, one or two old pans, a knife, a couple of sets of new feedsack sheets that my sister had made, and a few other things.

The apartments sat in a row like boxes. They had once been white, but the many sandstorms common to Sanders had changed that white look to more of a sandy color. The sandstorms had taken their toll, and it was apparent that the owner wasn't too concerned about fixing them up. There were four identical one-room apartments as I recall. Kitchen, living room, and bedroom were all together in a single room. They were open and airy.... very airy. I suspect the owner saw no need to do much insulating since he was the one who sold the heating fuel. There was one little house beside the apartments. It was a small four-room prefab house. I wondered who would be privileged to rent that little house.

I soon learned that another home economics teacher had been hired. I met her a day or two after I arrived. She was tall and attractive and prided herself on her sewing abilities. She loved to use Vogue Patterns which seemed a little out of place to me at that location. I began to wonder why two teachers had been hired for such a small school. It seems that the school had such a hard time getting teachers that they would hire more than one in case some backed out of coming. Then when they arrived, they would be used where needed, irregardless of training. As it happened, I was told to go ahead and teach home economics, and she was assigned a class in the elementary grades. She lived in the apartment next to mine, and we would carry our coffee cups to each other's apartment when we wanted to get together, since we each had only one cup. She and I spent a great deal of time together since we were the only single people around.

The school enrollment was made up of both Navajo and Anglo students, probably about fifty-fifty. Even though the enrollment was small, probably less than fifty in the high school and a hundred and fifty in the elementary school, it was still more than I thought it would be when I first saw Sanders. I soon learned that there were big ranches around as well as businesses strung along Route 66. Children were bussed in from many miles.

To this day, I question the wisdom of the principal and superintendent for assigning me as senior class sponsor. There were at least three male students in that class older than myself. Since Navajo children came in not knowing English, they were often put in a pre-first grade to learn English until they were ready to be put in first grade. Also, at that time, many of the Navajo children did not start to school until they were seven, eight, or nine years old, making them older than usual when they graduated. Since I was only twenty, I tried to think of ways to gain respect and hide my age. My high heels were my best resource. As long as I wore high heels, all of the students seemed to think of me as a teacher. If I ever took them off, there was a difference in their behavior.

My home economics classes were very small. That was nice. The superintendent informed me at the beginning of the year that there was money available for me to use to remodel the department. I had it painted, and ordered new cabinets, appliances, and sewing machines. It was shining! I started that first year of teaching full of big dreams and lots of enthusiasm. "Give me the biggest problem child and I will conquer all the problems of the student, teach that student, and make a wonderful citizen!" Teaching was my lifelong dream. I felt confident that I could be a great teacher!

It didn't take very long for me to realize that very little in my four years of college had prepared me for what I was dealing with. This little school was full of politics. Some of the kids had been let to get by with very unruly behavior. They bragged about having run off several teachers by throwing eggs on their cars and apartments. About six weeks into the year, the chemistry teacher left. The kids had thrown eggs on his car and ruined the chrome. He wanted nothing to do with this school. The principal came to me and told me that since I had more science training than any of the other teachers; I would have to teach the chemistry class in addition to my home economics classes. I felt completely inadequate. Of all things to teach, I would have to teach chemistry!

Those of us old enough recall that in the '50s, boys would sometimes comb their hair to a peak straight out in front of their foreheads. One boy in the chemistry class wore his hair this way and another student used the Bunsen burner and set fire to the point of hair. Thankfully, it only scorched the ends. Needless to say, we didn't have lab any more often than necessary. The students seemed to want big noises and bad smells!

I found that hardly ever did the Navajo children cause discipline problems. The rancher's kids, however, were a different story. I met a real challenge one day when covering a unit on dating in the family relations class. I told my girls a story that my family relations teacher in college told us and felt it would be helpful in getting the girls to understand the importance of waiting until marriage to experience sexual relationships. "When a girl doesn't keep herself from having premarital sex," I told them, "it is like when you go into the bargain basement of a department store and see a big sign on a table that says, 'Goods slightly soiled, price greatly reduced.'" The next day, my entire class showed up wearing a sign pinned on them that read "10 cents." I was stunned! Knowing that they were trying to upset me, I thought it best to simply ignore the signs and continue with the day's lesson. It was truly like an elephant in the room, but we got through the class with no comment about the signs. They did not wear the signs the next day.

Some mothers volunteered to help chaperone our FHA (Future Homemakers of America) girls to Flagstaff for a state FHA meeting. One of the girls, a very nice and deserving girl, was running for a state Future Homemakers of America office. Her friend had volunteered to make her campaign speech. One would have to look far to find a more conscientious and sweet girl than this friend who was so willing to volunteer to make the speech. She was so conscientious, in fact, that she wrote her speech weeks ahead of time and went over and over it. She was a timid and shy girl and worried incessantly about the speech she would have to make in front of so many people.

The time came for us to go to Flagstaff, to the big meeting we had so anticipated. We sat in the auditorium and listened to the speeches of others who were running for office. My candidate's mother leaned over to me and whispered her concerns that her daughter would not get elected. The wheels started turning in my mind. How could I save the situation? How could I get my candidate elected and not embarrass my conscientious little speech writer? We had only a couple of minutes until our turn came. I leaned over to my campaigner and whispered to her. I told her when it was her turn to make her speech, she should take off her high heels, and run as hard as she could to the stage in the big auditorium. Then, I told my candidate to run after her and yell, "Hey, where are you going?" Then she was to answer, "To vote for Ann!" Then she was to tell in her own words why they should vote for our girl. It worked! Our girl was elected and our campaigner had experienced success!

While in Flagstaff, we stayed in a local motel. I noticed that the mother of one of my girls was putting curlers in the hair of her daughter. Later, she took them out and combed her hair. I suspected this girl to be somewhat retarded. In sewing class, she would try to make the sewing machine go and stop at the same time. She was always very nervous. The records of the students were not available to us, and she was making good grades in all of her other classes. In my class, in spite of the extra help I was giving her, she was about to fail. One morning, I overheard her mother tell another mother, "I'm going to get her through high school if I have to pull her through by the hair of her head. That's why I got on the school board!" I felt so sorry for this girl who really needed to be in a situation where she could get special help. Special education classes were not available then. After hearing this comment, I understood why she was getting good grades in the other classes. I suspected that the teachers were afraid to grade her down, because her mother was on the school board. She barely passed my class. I suspected the mother had more respect for me. I'm sure she knew the daughter's true capabilities.

I was also assigned the job of being the cheerleader sponsor. It was necessary for me to drive my car and take the cheerleaders to the away games. There was always a great deal of driving. Nothing was close to anything else in northern Arizona. I got to know those girls pretty well, but not as well as I thought. I suppose I was stricter than most of the teachers and that bred resentment. It was those same girls who later threw eggs on my car.

As part of the vocational program, I made home visits to the homes of those students who did not live on the reservation. Since the school was right on the edge of the reservation, some of the Navajo girls lived in hogans. (Hogans are homes made of logs and mud in the shape of hexagons) I did not visit them because I could not find them. Many of them were on dirt roads traveled only by wagons or horses. Of course, there were no addresses.

As senior class sponsor, it was my responsibility to chaperone the senior class on their end of the year senior trip. They decided that they wanted to go to Roosevelt Dam near Tempe. They began talking a lot about the things that happened on senior trips in the past. It was apparent that they were trying to think of naughty things to do on their trip to earn bragging rights. Some of the seniors decided not to go on the trip. Since the class was small to begin with, this left only one carload to go, and I would be doing the driving. There was no way those kids were going to act out on my watch! I dogged their every move. I even knew how long it took them to go to the bathroom! I'm not sure they had very much fun on that trip, but they had no truthful bad stories to tell when they got back!

Toward the end of my first year, the superintendent came down to the home economics room and sat down to talk to me. He asked me if I knew a good place to stay in St. Louis. He said that he planned to go back there and interview potential teachers. He grinned and said that he was going to hire me a husband, so I wouldn't leave Sanders. I laughed and said, "All right. Go ahead!" I had dated the park ranger from the Petrified Forest and Painted Desert which were a little further down Route 66 a couple of times, but it had gone nowhere. A couple of people had tried to find dates for me, but single young men were simply not available in the area. I felt that God wanted me to stay another year. I completely dismissed from my mind what the superintendent had said and went on about my work. I signed a contract for the coming school year.

A few weeks later, the superintendent saw me and remarked that he had gone to St. Louis. "How did you do?" I asked jokingly, not dreaming that he had been serious about his earlier promise. "Well," he said, "I hired two single guys. One I don't know about, but the other one…maybe." Unfortunately, due to the local politics, he lost his contract and was not hired back for the coming year, so when a single music teacher and a single math teacher showed up the following fall, I didn't know which he thought was right for me. I have wondered in the years since which one he meant. It would be interesting to know.

Since I was the only woman on the high school faculty, it fell on my lot to always plan for coffee and dessert at staff meetings and to plan any other social activities for the staff. I planned a dinner for the faculty at the beginning of the school year. By this time, I had moved out of my little apartment and moved into a trailer in the yard of a widow who lived across the Puerco River from the school. She had a nice home and was more than glad to let us have the get-together there. Everyone brought something, and my contribution was a pumpkin pie. (To this day, Keith says he married me because I made such a good pumpkin pie and I have never made one the same way since!)

In all honesty, neither of the two single teachers impressed me. I thought it not possible that I could have graduated from

Mizzou where there was a ratio of seven to one, boys to girls, and come west to meet a future husband. However, the math teacher asked me to go to Gallup to a movie with him. (He now tells everyone that he and the music teacher flipped a coin to see who would ask me for a date first and that he lost!) It wasn't as though my social calendar was full, so I said yes. I felt comfortable and relaxed with him. He had played football in Nebraska and was all-state player in Nebraska for two years in high school. He had a brand new silver-colored Dodge. We soon found ourselves spending more and more time together. One day, Keith came to the house where I lived (I had by now moved into the house from the trailer), and told me he needed to talk to me. We went outside and sat on a rock wall and had a long talk. He told me that he had been engaged back at his home in Wymore, Nebraska, and had just broken it off. I wondered why he told me all of those things. I still had not thought of marriage at this point. I had made friends with a missionary couple who ran a children's home a few miles down the highway. She and I had become pretty close. I told her about our conversation, and she smiled and said, "Sounds like you are getting serious."

Keith was not what I had pictured my husband to be like, but I soon found that when he would leave me after we would be together, I had a lonely feeling. It seemed like part of me would be gone. It seemed so right when were together. We were relaxed with each other, and it seemed that I wanted to be with him all the time. We had met in August, and in October, he proposed to me. I said yes.

I had been praying about my answer prior to the proposal and asked God to stop me from marrying Keith if it was not his plan for me. I insisted that Keith should go talk to the pastor of the local church I had been attending. He had not been attend-ing church in college, but said he was a Christian. He attended church with me in Sanders. When he talked to the pastor, he asked, "How do you feel about hunting on Sundays?" The young pastor told him that he thought you could worship God in nature and that it was okay. He didn't get much help from this pastor who liked to witness by having a drink in the bar and socializing with people. I was more than a little disappointed. Since there was no other pastor around for him to talk to, I decided it was God's will for us to go ahead and marry.

The students at the school had been watching us with more than a little interest. They had to say something in almost every issue of the school paper about us. "Mr. Lamb went fishing Saturday night," they would write. In the next issue it might say, "Miss Haddock went sheepherding." We decided that since we were sure of what we wanted to do, we should get married as quickly as possible to stop all of the turmoil among the kids at school.

We decided that the home of our missionary friends would be the place to have the wedding. Elbert, the head of the home, could perform the ceremony. Keith wanted to wait until he went back to Nebraska at Christmas to buy my rings, so we would get married right after Christmas vacation. We traveled through the night to go to Missouri for Christmas where Keith left me and went on to Nebraska. I made my wedding dress during the vacation. When he came back, he gave me my engagement ring. It was beautiful! But we had a problem. A big storm was coming from the west and we thought it would not be right to be marooned in a snowstorm and not be married. We decided to get married in Verona. I caught the local Baptist preacher at the post office and asked him if he would marry us that afternoon. He agreed, and we were married in his parsonage. My sister Helene and her husband, Gene, were our witnesses. My family was somewhat taken aback with the whole thing and did not have time to even get ready and come. My mom, however, took the time to offer me some advice. She said, "Patsy, I'm going to tell you the same thing I told the other girls when they got married. When you have trouble getting along, and everyone does at some time or another, don't come home. Work it out between the two of you." It is interesting to note that none of my four sisters or I ever divorced.

Keith and I counted our way back to Sanders as our honeymoon. We stopped in Tulsa the first night, in Amarillo the second night, and arrived back in Sanders the next day. Keith and the other single teacher had been living in the only house available for teachers. It was the small prefab house I had noticed when I first arrived at Sanders. They had agreed that the first one of them to marry would get the house.

When we arrived there, Keith very gallantly carried me up the step (a large rock that had been placed at the end of the small porch) and into the house. He mentioned on the way that the last thing he had done before leaving for vacation was to pull the switch on the electric box to turn off the electricity so the electric bill would be lower. As soon as we walked in the door, I smelled a terrible odor. There was oil that had leaked from the old oil heater and about three-fourths of the living room carpet was saturated. When I opened the refrigerator door, blood was running down from the freezing compartment. He had forgotten about the venison he had put in the freezer when he turned off the electricity several days earlier. The rest of the house looked like one might expect it to look if two bachelors lived there. Later, the other single teacher laughed and told me, "We didn't care too much about cleaning. When one of us took a bath, we just filled the tub to the ring left by the last person! That way, we had only one ring in the bathtub!"

The early prefabricated houses had a lot of flaws, and this one was no exception. You could see daylight in the corner behind the kitchen stove where the two walls were supposed to come together. This house, too, was owned by the man who sold the fuel oil.

We had a couple of days before we had to be back in school. We went to the trading post and bought a large sack of flour and sprinkled it on the oil in the living room. We borrowed a vacuum cleaner from our missionary friends at the children's home and vacuumed it up. It helped some. Then I scrubbed and scrubbed on the rest of the house to do the best I could to make it a home.

It was so good to be able to count on Lael and Elbert Miller, the missionaries at the children's home, to always be there for help. Of course, it was my intention that I was to be a missionary and help the Indian people, but in all honesty, I wonder if the missionaries didn't help us more.

The Millers were affiliated with United Indian Missions headquartered in Flagstaff, Arizona. This was an organization that required its missionaries to raise their own support. This was a difficult task. The home was a renovated old, abandoned trading post…a work still in progress as long as we were in the area. Keith had majored in industrial arts and math, so he was able to help Elbert a small amount with some of the work. I spent some time in the kitchen helping Lael with the cooking. We became very close friends. Our love for serving the Lord was a bond between us. We did what we could spontaneously as needed. We gave our tithe money to the home and had a great many meals there. It was there that Keith first prayed aloud.

Each evening, as the children and the four of us sat around the dinner table, Elbert would go around the table and ask each person what they were thankful for. Next, he would go around the table and ask each person what they wanted to pray for. One evening, he called on Keith to lead the prayer. I don't think he knew that Keith had never prayed aloud. What could Keith do? Ten little pairs of eyes were looking at him in anticipation. They, too, had no idea that Keith had never prayed aloud. After an embarrassing pause, Keith cleared his throat and prayed! He did just fine.

Quite late one evening, we got a call from Elbert. He and Lael had been on deputation back East to raise money for the home. Of course, all of the children were with them. Usually, there was something wrong with the vehicles they had to use. Sure enough, their old Volkswagen bus had broken down in Grants, New Mexico, as they were coming back home. Keith called Homer Allen, and the two got in the pickup we now owned and went to help.

When they got there, neither they nor Elbert were able to get the vehicle to run, so they hitched it on the back of the pickup and started pulling it to Chambers. The children were looking out the windows of the VW bus and were spotted by the highway patrol. The patrolman told them that what they were doing was illegal. Towing a vehicle with people in it was not allowed. Now, what could they do? Somehow, they all piled in the pickup and continued to pull the broken-down vehicle home, all the time praying that they wouldn't be stopped for having too many in the pickup.

There was an older couple who also helped at the home. Mr. Allen owned an oil rig and was drilling for oil in the area. His wife, Oma, had a lot of time on her hands, so she spent much of it at the children's home. They gave a great deal of money to help when needed and became quite close to the Millers. Lael tells how she was sitting in the little church we attended one Sunday and put her last dollar in the offering plate. She didn't know the Allens at the time, but Oma was sitting in the pew behind her. As Lael put her last dollar in the plate, she prayed, "Lord, you promised to provide." After church, Oma approached Lael and told her that even though she didn't know her, the Lord had impressed upon her to give some money to Lael. Oma wrote a check and gave it to Lael.

Since the home was located on the very edge of the Navajo Reservation, word had spread for a distance that missionaries lived there. This meant that occasionally some of the Navajo people would come for help. On one occasion, while we were at the children's home, there was a knock on the front door. It was a Navajo lady who had walked there from somewhere on the reservation carrying her dead baby. She did not speak English, but

Keith and Elbert figured out that she had brought the baby for burial. Keith and Elbert dug a grave in the corner of the back yard and conducted a short graveside funeral.

Of the children at the home, the ones I most remember were Monty, Lester, and Angelita. Lael and Elbert saw to it that all of the children had chores assigned according to their capabilities. Lester was a big help to Elbert as his "gopher." He would "gopher" whatever tool or other thing Elbert might need. Angelita was a big help to Lael in the kitchen. These were the two older children. They had very sweet personalities. Monty was about nine years old and a real clown. He knew how to put an innocent, "Who? Me?" look on his face whenever he got in trouble. Elbert and Lael poured their hearts into the children to help them become the best they could be. It is sad to say that things did not turn out as hoped. Lester became a park ranger when he grew up and was thought to be doing well, but then someone found that he had committed suicide. Monty became an alcoholic and was killed. Angelita was diagnosed with cancer and passed away. We never heard the details of how the other children turned out.

In spite of the excitement of getting married, that school year was very tough. A few incidents led up to one of the most devastating things that ever happened to either Keith or me.

During the football season, someone threw eggs on my car and the place where I was living. Having gone to the new superintendent and principal, and getting absolutely no backing or action, Keith and I went to the county juvenile officer in St. Johns, Arizona. He was very cooperative and came to the school and investigated. He called students in, one at a time, and questioned them. He finally found out that the cheerleaders were the guilty ones. For punishment, he made them wash my car during an afternoon football game behind the bleachers where all of the other kids could see them. Needless to say, this did not set well with the students. One might think that the administration would be glad to have the egg-throwing stopped, but this didn't seem to be the case. Rather, they were upset that we had gone to the juvenile officer.

Another incident occurred when one of Keith's students misbehaved. Keith gave a quiz in his geometry class every Friday. One of the brighter students would not study. One Friday, the student wadded up his test paper, threw it in the trash and called Keith a son-of-a-bitch. Keith took him to the office, and he was suspended for three days. His father, a rancher in the area, came to the school to see Keith and threatened to beat him up. Keith responded by saying, "Maybe you can, but no one has ever done that before, and I promise you that we will tear up a lot of ground in the process!" The father lunged across the principal's desk at Keith, and the principal separated them. After that, the student did his studying and did much better in class. The father had threatened to take care of Keith outside of school but never made an attempt to do so. Keith was an all-state football player in Nebraska for two years when he was in high school. After seeing Keith, he may have thought differently.

Another incident occurred when I was summoned to the office one day because the financial manager of the school wanted to talk to me. His daughter had failed in her home economics class because she would not hand in homework or make any effort to study. He insisted that I give her a better grade and pass her so she could graduate. "I do not give grades," I told him. "I simply write down what the students do and hand it back to them." He got red in the face and told me, "I can make it difficult, if not impossible, for you to get a job anywhere in the state of Arizona if you don't change her grade!" I told him I would not change her grade but would be willing to tutor her in a home-decorating class since she seemed to have an interest in that area. It would mean that I would be teaching a special class just for her, but

I would be willing to make the lesson plans, assignments, and grade her work if she wanted to do that.

The student came to me and asked me if I would help her with a decorating class. I did so. It meant a great deal more work for me, but I was more than happy to help her. She did very well with decorating. At the end of the year, she and her mother came to see me and gave me a beautiful set of turquoise and silver bracelets to show their appreciation. However, her father was rather cool to me from our meeting on.

We speculate, as we look back, that these incidents led to our big devastating disappointment. We had taken the teaching positions with high ideals, wanting to make positive contributions to the education of our students. Nothing we had in college even came close to preparing us for the challenges we faced in our efforts to help the youngsters. Strangely enough, most of our friends thought it would be hard to teach Indian children. Actually, our Navajo children caused us very little grief. It was the children of the ranchers who did most of the harm. In our own minds, we felt that we had done a good job. During my two years there, I remodeled the home economics department, started a Future Homemakers of America club, had a state officer for the club elected, had been chosen to help chaperone the state FHA delegation to Chicago, had been published in the national *Practical Home Economics* magazine, and felt confident that I had helped several girls have a better understanding of homemaking. With the exception of the one student who gave him trouble, Keith felt that he had accomplished quite a bit. His geometry class prepared a topographical map on a large piece of plywood demonstrating how to determine the width of a river or lake by using geometry. It was entered in the science fair in St. Johns, Arizona, and the class took first place. However, when it came time to offer new contracts for the following school year, we were not offered contracts! We were told by the superintendent that we had been late coming back from lunch for class. Actually, I had prided myself on using my homemaking skills to be able to have our lunch prepared so that we would always be on time for our next class. On the other hand, we had noticed that other teachers were often ten to fifteen minutes late for their classes, and sometimes, teachers would sit in the office talking to the superintendent and leave their classes unattended!

I can't describe how heartbroken I was. To try as hard as we did and accomplish what we did, and then be told that we were rejected for fabricated reasons was a hard thing to take. It is no wonder that so many teachers quit teaching. But I could not quit teaching. From first grade, I had planned to teach. There we were, two newlyweds, and not the faintest idea of what we would do.

Mr. Willingham, a retired Baptist preacher, had come to Sanders to follow the Lord's will. His wife taught in the elementary school. He tried to comfort us by saying, "You know, sometimes getting kicked out means getting kicked up in God's sight." He was a real comfort. Keith and I have often commented that if that hadn't happened, we might have stayed there accomplishing little because of restrictions. It was God's way of moving us on. One of my faults has always been to hang on too long to something. I guess it is a stubborn streak in me!

Someone told us about the Bureau of Indian Affairs. There was an office in Gallup about forty miles away. We were told that there were Indian schools on the Navajo reservation. We had enjoyed our work with the Indian students for the most part, and I still felt that God wanted me to be a missionary. Maybe this was what God wanted.

In the meantime, the director of United Indian Missions in Flagstaff had told our missionary friends at the children's home about an opening for a home economics teacher at Window Rock, Arizona, in the public school there. I applied for that job, and the school was getting ready to offer both of us teaching contracts. I had some symptoms that indicated that there might be a little lamb on the way. We went to see a doctor at Ganado Mission. The doctor thought I was right in thinking there might be a baby coming. When the administration at Window Rock found out, they did not issue a contract. Their need had been for a home economics teacher and since they assumed I wouldn't be able to teach since I was pregnant, they did not extend the contract. The missionary friend was on the school board there and told us all that transpired. Later, we found out that I was not pregnant, but they had already decided to hire someone else by the time we found out. Once again, God was directing our paths!

We went to Gallup and talked to the man in charge of hiring for the Bureau of Indian Affairs. "Yes," he told us. "We need teachers on the reservation." He didn't know for sure where we would be assigned, and the government did not use contracts. We had only a handshake and even that didn't seem very certain. We had no other alternative at the moment, so we trusted him. He did not give us very much information, and we didn't know what to ask. We thought we would be living in a hogan somewhere on that big Navajo reservation which is approximately the size of West Virginia. Since Keith was a math and industrial arts major, and I had majored in home economics, we talked about how he could build furniture, and I would make curtains and slipcovers. We could fix up a hogan and would be an example for the Navajo people to know how to fix up their homes. We actually thought that we would be living in a hogan. We even talked about how to deal with the dirt floor and how to disinfect it and get all the bugs out since we knew that many of the children had lice.

Keith made an oak couch, and I made the cushions for it. As it turned out, however, we were assigned to live in government quarters at Lukachukai, Arizona, and the quarters were furnished. We were to have the title of teachers-guidance. Keith was to be in charge of a dormitory of third and fourth graders; I was to be in charge of a dormitory of first and second graders at the boarding school there.

We were off to a new adventure at Lukachukai, Arizona!

All on a Handshake

We had experienced a taste of the reservation while at Sanders, since Sanders was located on the edge of the reservation. Now, we were going to really find out what the Navajo people and the Navajo reservation were like!

It had taken us most of the summer to get all of the paperwork done and jump through all the hoops to become government workers for the Bureau of Indian Affairs. We had been fingerprinted and investigated as was required of all government employees. We spent a great deal of the summer helping our missionary friends at the children's home. They had other friends nearby who helped support the home monetarily. This was Homer and Oma Allen. Homer was the man who had gone with Keith the night Elbert phoned with the broken-down Volkswagen bus. The man in this family ran an oil rig and Keith worked on it part of the summer. That was a source of income since our teaching contracts had expired. As it turned out, it was also an educational experience for Keith.

In the Southwest, the humidity is very low. When mud is pumped into a pit while drilling, often, the top part will dry out, but underneath is soft, gooey mud. It must be a standing joke to send new workers to get something on the opposite side of the pit. This is what they did to Keith. Since the top part is hard, one naturally thinks that you can walk on it. Alas! As soon as Keith stepped on it, down into the mud pit he went. Everyone had a good laugh except Keith and me. I didn't enjoy washing his clothes!

Finally, we were satisfied that we actually did have a job, and we began to prepare to move to Lukachukai. It took faith to move without an actual contract, but that is the way it was done. We loaded our few belongings in our '54 Dodge pickup truck. We had been surprised to find out that we would be living in government quarters that were furnished. Since we wouldn't need the furniture that we had made, we gave it to the children's home. We still had the '57 Ford that I had bought, but Keith had sold his silver-colored Dodge. We had decided when we married that we didn't need two cars and would sell the first one we had an offer on. Keith's car was newer and more attractive, I suppose, and it went first. We had purchased the used pickup to use in remote areas. Keith drove the pickup, and I drove the Ford.

"Go to the end of the world, and then go fifty miles further," someone told us. "There is Lukachukai!"

We left Chambers from the children's home where we had been helping, and headed almost straight north to Ganado Mission, then Chinle, and on to Many Farms. The only black-top was between Ganado and Many Farms. On dirt road, we went about thirty-five miles further through the red clay hills and Round Rock and on to Lukachukai.

The road to Ganado was somewhat familiar, but we hadn't been further on the reservation than that. Rattlesnake Flats, a name given by locals for the area between Chambers and Ganado, was well named. There were lots of sidewinder rattlesnakes on the reservation. The Navajo people didn't believe in killing them. If one crawled into their area, they would simply move it out of their area back to its place among the sagebrush and other vegetation.

This trip was simply reinforcing my first impression of the reservation. My impression was that the reservation was a great big expansion of nothingness! As far as you looked, you could actually see nothing but sagebrush or rabbitbrush, but no trees or houses. What a change from my green Missouri and Keith's Nebraska! Occasionally, a dirt road would lead off the main road to a hogan that blended into the horizon almost completely obscure. The dirt roads had deep, deep ruts from wagon wheels or pickup trucks having driven in the mud during an occasional rain. Some roads had ruts as deep as hubcaps on the pickup trucks. There was no passing on these roads. They were for one vehicle only. The ditches beside the road had lots of sand in them, and here and there were miniature sand dunes where the wind had piled the sand during the terrible sandstorms so common in the area.

Ganado Mission was a Presbyterian mission that had been established years before. There were actually trees there! They were old giant cottonwood trees. The hospital there served many people in the surrounding area. There was no grass surrounding the buildings. Sand was everywhere. It would have been a gigantic chore to try to keep grass watered. At any time, one could see real people here. There would be Navajo ladies in their long *squaw* skirts, velvet blouses, and turquoise jewelry and men in their cowboy hats or no hats at all. The older men often wore a scarf as a headband and many had wrapped cloth around a long bun of hair in the back. Most of the men wore jeans and western shirts. Some older men wore moccasins. Most of the younger men wore cowboy boots. Many of the younger women would be carrying babies in a cradleboard. Ganado was like an oasis.

It was about fifty miles, as I recall, from Ganado to Chinle. Canyon de Chelly is located at Chinle. Our agency office was also located at Chinle. We stopped there to meet the agency superintendent, Miss Minnie Gould. She was Anglo, and it was apparent that she was very competent in her work. She had a look in her eyes of a strict schoolmarm. We felt that we should be very careful in the way we talked to her. Keith was much braver than I. He actually asked her if he would be allowed to take off work to go deer hunting! She looked directly at him and said slowly and deliberately, "Mr. Lamb, if I let the men off to go deer hunting,

I would have to let all the women off to get their hair fixed." He knew his answer!

Many Farms was about fifteen miles past Chinle. There was a gas station there, but as you can imagine, the prices were high compared to off-reservation prices. A building or two were near the gas station that was operated by Anglo men. Anglo people operated the trading posts and other businesses on the reservation. There is not much more that can be said about Many Farms. I'm not sure of how the name came about unless at one time there had been small patches of corn grown there.

Shortly after leaving Many Farms, we came to the red clay hills. This was the southernmost part of Monument Valley, and there were beautiful rock formations there, as well as portions that looked like the Painted Desert. The dirt road ran through a low flat place and crossed a dry ravine. One had to wonder about a bridge and a dry ravine, but we later learned that during flash floods, the ravine could contain much water. The road wound up the side of one of the formations. It was a little wider than a one-lane road and looked as though it were completely red clay. When we finally got to the top, we could see a water tower and a group of buildings huddled together. We knew that had to be Round Rock, named for the round rock visible from the little settlement. A government school was located here.

The road bypassed Round Rock. About sixteen miles further was Lukachukai. We were almost there! After passing a windmill with a tank of water beside it, we headed down and then up a little hill to our destination.

Lukachukai was situated at the bottom of the Chuska Mountain Range. On the other side of the mountain was Shiprock, New Mexico. The trail over the mountain was not passable most of the time. Once or twice during the summer, the brave dared to attempt it. The "road" was terrible. In the winter, the snow covered the mountains, so it was definitely impassable then. In the summer, the ruts were so deep and rocks and limbs from trees were in the road. However, the road was passable for a small distance at the bottom of the mountain, and we would find it alluring on our days off to go to a little picnic area by a bubbling brook. Big ponderosa pine trees were there and it looked, for all the world, like a scene from the Colorado Rockies. We went there many times for our "Navajo Businessman's Luncheon" of bologna sandwiches, chips, pop, and little pies. On occasion, we would go to the trading post, purchase a loaf of bread, a jar of sandwich spread, a package of bologna, and other things. We would go and sit at the picnic table to enjoy hearing the wind whistle through the pines and the sound of running water in the brook. It was nice!

South of Lukachukai, we could see Tot-tso (big water) canyon. The Navajo people in the area gave the canyon this name because it rained there so much. In August, almost every day, we could see a cloud come and form over the canyon. The sun would be shining all around us, but we would watch it rain in that canyon. What an unusual phenomenon!

To the north of the school campus were the beautiful red bluffs that jutted out from the mountains. Sometimes, they were red; sometimes, they were bright orange; and sometimes, they would have purple and blue hues as the sun would begin to set, until finally, they would turn black in the dark of night. They were so very beautiful! They offered peaceful solace to all who were fortunate enough to see them, and we realized that we were part of the few who would ever witness their profound beauty.

The campus itself had four main buildings and several smaller buildings including quarters for workers there. One building housed the classrooms and office of the principal. There was a separate building for the kitchen and dining room. There were two dormitories built to house sixty students in each of the two wings of each dorm. If you imagine a capital L turned backwards and another one upside down with the bases overlapping, you can picture the shape of the dormitories. One of the Ls was the boys' wing and the other was the girls' wing. There were isolation rooms at the end of each wing to isolate children when they had a contagious disease such as measles. (This was before the measles vaccine was used.) Apartments for workers were on the end of the wings beyond the isolation rooms. We usually had more than the 120 students in each dorm that they were designed to house. Somehow, we managed to get more beds in as needed.

In addition to the main buildings, there was an old Collier's building or two on campus. (Collier's buildings were old buildings built during the time that John T. Collier had worked for the government. They were made of stone.) These were used for the clinic and a classroom. The public health doctor came up from Chinle one time each week to see the sick children and we would take them to the clinic. There was another small building for the diesel machine that made electricity for the campus. Electricity had not yet come to the reservation and all electricity for the campus was provided by a diesel generator. (That meant that a lot of light bulbs were required as they burned out often.) There were a few buildings for quarters. The principal had the largest quarters, but older. The house was similar to the Collier's buildings as it, too, was made of stone. There were two rows of apartments for teachers and staff. There was also a small house that was located near the girls' dorm.

The dorms, kitchen, apartments, and office building were just a few years old. The tile in the dorms was cracking and it was said that cheap tile was used by the contractor who thought it didn't matter since it was for the government. There was a bucket or two of broken pieces of tile saved to show the contractor. It was said that some men had come to examine the floor several times, would take a tool and pry the tile and say they agreed that the tiles were not good. Where they checked, more pieces would break off and be added to the buckets. They never got around to actually doing anything about it.

Just down the hill from the school campus was the Catholic mission. At one time, the Navajo government had decided that because there were so many missionaries from different denominations that they would simply divide the reservation between them. Lukachukai was in the Catholic part. The Catholics claimed that 98 percent of the people at Lukachukai were Catholic. We knew, however, that many of the people were members of the Native Church of North America. This Native Church included the peyote users. Peyote is a hallucinatory drug that is abundant in Texas. It is the bloom of a plant. The users of peyote say that when they use it, they can hear a whisper across the room. Some also claim that they can see Jesus and talk directly to him. Our government has made its use legal for Native Americans since they claim it is used in a religious ceremony.

When we arrived at the campus, we went to the office and met Mr. James Bearghost, the principal. He introduced us to a gentleman who was in charge of the dormitories but was transferring to another location. This gentleman proceeded to take us on a tour of the campus. After we saw the dorms, he said, "I want to take you down to the Catholic church since it is really a part of our school." I was thinking about the separation of church and state, but I didn't say anything. We went ahead and toured the church and met the priest and nuns. It was made very clear to us that we were to cooperate with the Catholic mission in every way.

A week or two after our arrival, we attended an orientation of new employees at the agency office in Chinle. At this meeting, an Indian gentleman told us a story that made a real impact on me. He said there were two people who went to the grave of a friend on Memorial Day. One of the persons was white, the other Indian. It happened that the graves of their friends were side by side. The white man put flowers on the grave of his friend and looked over to see the Indian man putting food on the grave of his friend. The white man began to laugh and said, "When do you think your friend is going to come up and eat that food?" The Indian man looked at him and calmly said, "Maybe the same time your friend comes up to smell and see those flowers." This was a real lesson to me that basically people are all the same. They may have physical differences and they may express their emotions in different ways, but God can be real to all and Jesus came to die for all.

Our official title was teacher-guidance. Our position descriptions required us to oversee the care of the children, make sure the buildings were clean, and give a guidance lesson each evening. We each had thirteen to fourteen instructional aids to supervise. One of the workers "floated" between dorms. We had to make out the work schedules for the aides, and it worked out so that we needed to have one worker split his/her time between the two dormitories.

One of the immediate concerns was the fact that children had been running away from the dormitories. We were told that in the previous year, two children had run away and had frozen their feet. Keith and I decided that the first thing we needed to do was make sure the children didn't run away for safety's sake, and then, we would concentrate on making them not want to run away.

All of our instructional aids were Indian. Some were Navajo, and some were from other tribes who had found employment in the Bureau of Indian Affairs. The Navajo aides were often able to discern which children might be at risk for running away. At night, we would hide the clothes of those children and watch them very carefully. We had a night attendant on each night in each dorm and Keith and I would make spot checks at random times through the night to see that all was well. We heard much complaining by the day aids that the night attendants were not doing enough ironing, etc. Not to be outdone, the night attendants complained that the day aids left too much work for them! We wanted the night attendants to watch the children first. They had to take and record the temperature of the sick children…and there were almost always sick children! Some nights we posted aides at each end of the dorm so the children could not sneak out without being caught.

We still had a few runaways. On one occasion a fourth grader had just moved back to the reservation from Phoenix. He ran away from class and did not walk back to the dorm with the other children. Keith saw him take off and he ran after him. The little boy could really run fast. Keith chased him over a hill or two and saw a sheepherder with a horse. Keith asked if he could borrow the horse. The sheepherder told him he could, but not to run it. Keith said that as soon as he got out of sight, he had the horse go fast enough to catch the boy and caught him just before he reached his home.

We had one boy who had a reputation for causing problems. He was in Keith's dorm. When he checked in, he hid in the locker. He didn't talk to the children, but would always keep to himself. He would run away over and over. One of the Navajo aids would track him. He told us that the boy would drag brush over his tracks and walk backwards to keep from being trailed. It seemed that no one could get through to him. One time, he got sick and was taken to the hospital in Fort Defiance, near Window Rock. He disappeared, and no one could find him. The hospital staff was upset because he couldn't be located. Someone went to his home to see if he had gotten there. He wasn't there. After several days, they found him in the ceiling of his hospital room. He had moved one of the large tiles in the ceiling and had been hiding up there all the time. They were exasperated not only from his hiding, but his constant erratic behavior. He had taken slats out of Venetian blinds and thrown them out the window, tried to run away, and was over all a real challenge to the staff.

The public health nurse made arrangements for this boy to go to Phoenix to see a psychologist. After the trip, the nurse told us that this boy had lived with a deaf grandmother all of his life and had helped herd sheep. He didn't know how to talk since he had not been around people who talked. This meant that he didn't know either the Navajo language or English. No wonder he was so frustrated!

The summer after we first met this boy, Keith and I were fishing in Wheatfields Lake. The old Navajo belief was that of reincarnation, we were told, and they did not eat fish because they were afraid it might be a relative! Keith and I enjoyed going fishing there because the state fish and game department stocked the lake with trout that were just pan-size. Keith had received a set of hand-tied flies as a gift from our doctor friend in Columbia that I had babysat for in college. He had bought a fancy fly rod and was sure he was going to catch a lot of fish. This troubled boy saw us and came over to where we were fishing. His grandmother's hogan was near the lake where he could easily see us. When he came over, I handed him the fishing rod I was using so he could fish. (He did not know about the reincarnation belief, I suspect.) I went to the car, opened the trunk, and found a broken rod that the trunk lid had been slammed on. I found some salmon eggs and some fireballs. I tied a string on the rod with a granny knot, put a hook and sinker on, and went to the lake to fish. I stood beside Keith on a little dock that had been built out into the water. I caught thirty-two fish and Keith caught two. Every time I would pull one out, our troubled boy would laugh. He could sense Keith's frustration and was enjoying himself watching Keith take my fish off the hook. Keith says he didn't get to fish much because he had to take my fish off for me. At any rate, our troubled boy was truly enjoying watching the two of us. I suspect we were good therapy for him!

Although we did have some runaways, none of them ever got hurt. We started buying toys for the children. We put a sliding board and merry-go-round and swings on the campus. One day, I looked out the window of my office and saw a mother sliding down the sliding board in her squaw skirt and velvet blouse, turquoise jewelry, and silver concho belt. She was checking out the sliding board to see what it was. Many of the parents examined the equipment and discussed its safety. We bought roller skates and balls. Keith taught his boys how to play softball. They had never played or seen softball before. The children never learned to skate with two skates. One child would put one foot on one skate and sit on the foot and hold the other foot off the ground. Another child would push the first child. They loved to do this!

We tried to make the children happy, and at the same time, maintain discipline. We had very few discipline problems. The children were very obedient. They lined up to go to school; they lined up to go to the dining hall; they lined up to go to church. They knew what to do, and they did it. One evening, when I was off duty, I looked out our window and watched the line of children walk to the dining hall. All of the little black-haired heads were about the same height. Then, I noticed a little head much lower to the ground walking in line with the children. We found out it was a little four-year-old girl who had run away from home to come to school! We felt we had succeeded in our plan to deal with runaways!

We understood how difficult it was for parents and children to be separated, but it seemed that there was no other way to educate the children for the future they faced. Parents were allowed to check out their children one time each month. On checkout day, the horse-drawn wagons would come with a dog or two trailing behind. The dogs found the trash cans at the school more lucrative than the scraps they got at home, and many chose to stay on campus. Too many dogs became a problem. Some of the men found a way to deal with it.

One time each month, the children could be checked out on a Friday and would come back on Sunday. The bad part about this procedure was that many of the children came back with head lice. Every Saturday morning, those with head lice would be called to the laundry room in each wing and the instructional aides would use fine combs and medicine to work on their heads. It was a familiar site to see children sitting on the floor and another person parting hair and carefully looking for nits and lice. Sometimes, some children would work on other children. The children would just about be rid of the lice when it was time for them to go home on checkout weekend again. When they went home, they would sleep on sheepskin rugs on a dirt floor in their hogans. I'm sure the sheepskin rugs were infested with lice. I was so glad that the instructional aids did this job, and I didn't have to do it. Sometimes, I would pass the laundry room and one of the aids would say, "Look, Mrs. Lamb, she has lots of nits!" I would give a nod and go on my way. It didn't keep me from giving hugs to the children, however. It seemed like hugs were a natural thing to do. I often got strep throat or tonsillitis. It may have been that I was contacting it by giving the children hugs.

Saturday mornings were haircut days for the boys. Keith did a lot of the haircuts with the help of some of the men aides. One day, he and the boys decided they would like to have Mohawk cuts. He gave some of the boys the Mohawk cuts, and they thought it was great fun. The priest, along with some of the parents and workers didn't think it was so funny, and Keith got a little reprimand for it. The hair finally grew out and all was forgotten.

The children looked forward to their checkout times. The parents could visit the children at any time through the month. They often did so, and in the fall, they would bring melons, apples, or other fruit they had grown for the children. The children could often be seen behind the dorm enjoying their fruit. There was a problem with this in that the children often got diarrhea. One time, the public health nurse was talking to the parents at the chapter house. (Chapter houses were scattered throughout the reservation. They were somewhat like town halls. The people would gather there to conduct business for the local community.) The nurse told the people that they should boil their *bell-a-ga-nas* before they ate them. The word for apples is *bell-a-sa-na*. The word for white people is *bell-a-ga-na*. She had told them to boil their white people before they ate them! That story had remained a good joke for quite some time.

As the children learned the English language, they often confused the times to use certain terms or words. Some children got the idea that to checkout meant to always go get someone. One day, some of the boys in Keith's dorm came to our apartment, located on the end of that dorm, and knocked on the door. When I answered it, they asked if they could check out Mr. Lamb to come and play with them! Keith played with the children a lot, and they would cling to him and liked to be around him. They were fascinated by the hair on his arms. Some would sit beside him and make fuzz balls with the hair on his arms by rubbing their hands in circles. They thought that was funny. The Indian people did not have that much hair on their arms, and it was a fascination to them.

We planned parties for the children and tried to do all we could to help them learn and make them happy. We thought of them as our own children. Occasionally, parents would come and try to take their children out of school. They would say they needed them at home to herd sheep. Not all parents were convinced that education was a good thing. It was understandable, too, that they simply missed their children.

On one occasion a mother, father, and grandmother came to take a little girl out of school. They were in my office, and I was trying to convince them of the importance of an education. My interpreter was Johnny Kinsel, a man who had been a code-talker in WWII. It took a long time to talk to parents because he had to interpret everything they said to me and everything I said to them. I really wished I could speak Navajo because it seemed like I would say a little and he would go on and on. Sometimes, he would tell me of thoughts he had interjected himself. I knew that the language is a language that goes into detail and paints pictures of things, but I often questioned what he was really telling them. On this occasion, we had talked for over an hour with me doing all I could to convince them that the child should stay in school. At last, when I was thoroughly exhausted, the grandmother who had been standing quietly in the back spoke up and said in good English, "That's right! Everything she says is right!" I was glad that she agreed, but she could have saved us lots of time if she had spoken up earlier. All the time, I had believed that she couldn't speak English! It was especially good to have the grandmother's opinion, since the Navajos were a matriarchal society, and the grandmother was considered the authority. The little girl stayed in school.

We were not allowed to spank the children nor did we seldom want to do so. Since Keith and I did not have children of our own, we pretty much thought of these children as ours and wanted the best for them. There was one child, however, who, in my opinion, needed a spanking. It was a sad situation, but I learned from this young boy the importance of treating handicapped people as you would treat other people. This young boy had lost some of his hearing due to ear infections as a small child. He had been in hospitals for surgery to put in artificial ear drums. He had apparently never been disciplined. The public health nurse gave us his history and as she worked with him, it was obvious that she was not expecting him to behave. I felt that she was letting her sympathy for him affect the way she treated him. I suspected that the nurses in the hospitals had felt the same way. He was spoiled! He spoke his limited English in a garbled way due to his inaccurate hearing as a child. One thing he had down really well in English was, "No, Lamb!" Every time I would ask him to do something, the response I got was, "No, Lamb!" When the other children would walk in line, he would saunter from side to side, just daring anyone to say anything. When it was bedtime, he would not go to bed. I would always get the same reply. It was apparent that his teacher at school was letting him get by with this behavior as was the nurse. It was natural that many would feel sorry for "that poor little Indian boy" and baby him a lot.

One night at bedtime, he refused to go to bed, and I got the usual, "No, Lamb." Keith had given me an idea that I decided to try. When all the other children were in bed, I took him in my office. I drew a line on the floor with chalk and drew a circle on the wall with chalk. I had him stand tiptoe on the line, hands behind his back, with his nose in a ring on the wall. I explained to him that when he obeyed me, he could stop standing that way. I was sure he understood what I meant and every little bit I would test him to see if he would obey. I knew that standing like this would only strengthen his calf muscles and could not really hurt him. Finally after several attempts to stop, he realized that he would have to obey. I asked him if he was ready to obey and he shook his head yes. I said, "Dale, wiggle your finger." I patterned the movement for him to follow, and he did so. I gave him a couple more small commands which he readily followed. From that time forward, we had no trouble with Dale.

About a month later, Dale's classroom teacher came to the dorm all excited and waving a letter of commendation from the public health nurse. The nurse had commended her for the great job she had done with this boy and remarked about his drastic change in behavior. Later, the nurse, too, commented to me about what a good job his classroom teacher had done and how he had changed. I kept quiet. Only Keith and I knew what had transformed him!

Government boarding schools throughout the reservation were set up to have a department head over dormitories. A department head/guidance, Miss Rodman, was assigned to our school. I thought Keith and I were doing just fine without one, but the powers that be decided to fill the vacant position. There were two offices, one in each dorm, but now we had three people who needed offices. She chose to take my office and a desk was placed in the linen room for me. She had been a WAC (Women's Army Corp) and had the demeanor of a sergeant. That was a hard time for me, but it was obvious she liked Keith. At the Christmas party, Keith dressed up like Santa. She rubbed arms with him and softly said, "This is the first time I've seen a blue-eyed Santa." Keith laughed about it.

The office in the linen room was not too bad for some things. The Navajo tribe bought clothing for the children, and we had to measure each child and send in the order. The children would come to the linen room for me to measure. Then, a few weeks later, large boxes of dresses, jeans, and shoes would arrive from Window Rock for the children. I'm not sure how much good it did to measure, for when the clothing arrived, it didn't seem to match the sizes I had sent in. It was nice that the tribe did this, but we heard that the teenagers at the Intermountain Boarding

School in Utah resented the clothing. We were told that they called the clothes "stogie clothes" and they burned the new clothes. This, in my opinion, was an illustration that individuals do not want *things* as much as they want respect.

A public health doctor and nurse came to the small clinic one time each week. We kept health charts on any sick children and would take them to the clinic when they came. If the children got sick in between visits, we had to take them to the clinic at Chinle, fifty miles away, or to Window Rock, about sixty-two miles away on dirt road. Our department head and I were walking to the clinic one day with the sick children, and she told me that she had been having a pain in her left shoulder and arm. I suggested she might tell the doctor since he was there that day. She said, "Oh, no. I'm Christian Scientist, and I believe that if I tell myself that I am okay that it will go away. It is a matter of mind control." I didn't think much more about it. When Christmas vacation came, she went to Indianapolis. While there, she had a heart attack and passed away.

Her father lived in Albuquerque and called to request someone bring her belongings to him. We had a pickup at the time and it became Keith's task to take the things to him. We had had a big snowstorm during the Christmas holiday season. Keith decided to cut through by Sawmill and Wheatfields Lake and go through Window Rock to save time. By taking this road, he would cut off more than fifty miles. Big mistake! Snow was thawing and refreezing. There were deep ruts and lots of mud. The mud was splashing up all over the truck and onto the windshield. He had no water to wash the windshield and couldn't see. If he put his head out the window, then his head would get covered in mud. Finally, he thought of a solution. He stopped the truck, stood up on the edge, and urinated on the windshield! Is that being resourceful, or what? He was able to get her belongings on to Albuquerque, and finally, got back to Lukachukai.

Our department head had lived in the little house that everyone kind of envied next to Dorm A. (Dorm A was the dorm for the younger children that I supervised.) After she passed away, the Navajo instructional aides were afraid of the house where she had lived. They called it a *chindegon* (chin-de-gon). This meant "devil house." The old custom of the Navajo was to burn a hogan when someone died in it. Even though she had not died in the house, I watched one day as one of our Navajo instructional aides walked a wide circle around the house on her way home. She would not go near it. For several months, the aides seemed very nervous around our sick children.

After the department head passed away, we were given the privilege of living in the little house and not having to live at the end of the dormitory. It was a welcome change. We attempted to landscape it and even built a small goldfish pond in the back. Some said, "Why do you bother planting flowers and landscaping? You may just have to move away and leave it." We thought that if everyone felt that way, there would never be any landscaping. We always tried to improve the houses where we lived. Our efforts with the goldfish pond were futile, though. The concrete cracked and the little pond filled with sand from the sandstorms.

We had so much wind and sand there! When you opened a door, you could feel the grittiness of sand in the doorknob. We actually had to shovel the sand out of the dorms at times. When the children would come back to the dorms from the classrooms, we would have to hold the door against the wind so they could get in. At these times, the sand would come in as well. It seemed that the sandstorms were worse in the spring. On one occasion, I was bracing myself against the wind and holding the door for the little ones to get in when one little boy looked up at me and said, "Mrs. Lamb, spring is here?" How sad, I thought. Back home in Missouri the first sign of spring was a robin. Here, the first sign of spring was a sandstorm!

Living in such an isolated area and such severe weather necessitated a dependable vehicle. My faithful '57 Ford was getting some age and lots of miles. We decided we had better trade it off and buy a new car that we could depend on. We went to

Rico Motor Company in Gallup and bought a brand new F85 Oldsmobile. We both felt good knowing that we had a new car that we could depend on when driving those lonely, long trips. We proudly headed for home after loading up the groceries.

Shortly after we passed Window Rock, one of the headlights went out and stopped working. Now, there were no street lights on the reservation. There was not even electricity on the reservation. It was very dark! Keith stopped the car and lifted the hood. A wire was dangling loose that apparently had barely been connected. Well, we thought, that shouldn't be too hard to fix. Keith thought he could probably fix it the next day when he had better light. In the meantime, we would just be careful and try to make it on home with the one headlight.

We continued on until we finally came to Round Rock. We were about fifteen miles from Lukachukai now. Suddenly, the heat gauge was showing that the engine was hot. Again, Keith got out, lifted up the hood, and sure enough, the radiator was making a noise as though it were boiling. There was no water anywhere, but there were patches of snow on the ground. Keith grabbed some handfuls of snow and put them on the radiator to cool it down. We inched our way on to the windmill that we knew was located midway between Round Rock and Lukachukai. Although there was water, we didn't have anything to use to carry it. I can't remember for sure what we did, but I think maybe we emptied some groceries from a container that he could use to get some water for the radiator.

We finally made it home, unloaded the groceries, and went to bed thinking that surely all the bugs had been worked out of this new car by now. The next morning, Keith fixed the headlight and decided to start the car. The car would not start! He finally decided that the carburetor was not working right. He got a short piece of hose, siphoned some gas from the gas tank, poured the gas in the carburetor, and it started! This became a ritual. Every time we wanted to go someplace in the car, he had to siphon gas from the gas tank and pour it in the carburetor before the car would start.

It was a month before we could go back to Gallup, but when we went, you know we went back to the salesman who sold us the car! They did something to the carburetor and checked the headlight and radiator and assured us that now we had a perfect car.

The car ran without serious problems until Keith took it to the Grand Canyon area to go deer hunting. On the way back, a U-joint broke out in the middle of nowhere. That was the straw that broke the camel's back! We determined that on the next trip to Gallup, a different car would be bringing us home. After all, we needed a car we could depend on!

We lost money on that car! Once you drive a car out of the salesroom, it is a used car. There were no laws in place at that time to protect us. We bought a Buick Special. Thankfully, it turned out to be a good car. We decided that the Oldsmobile had been put together on the assembly line at four o'clock on a Friday afternoon when everyone was in a hurry to get home!

One has to know that if there are as many children as we had, there would be a lot of sickness. One weekend, our principal left Keith in charge as acting principal of the campus. There was no good government vehicle on campus at the time. The "carry-all," as we called it, was running off the generator. We had nine children who had pneumonia and needed badly to see the doctor in Chinle. There was no choice but for me to drive the children to the doctor. With the roads we had then, as I recall it was about fifty miles away. None of the instructional aides would ride with me because they were afraid some of the children would die. When asked to go with me, they would duck their heads and not answer. I knew it was futile to keep trying to persuade them. I studied the charts of the children to determine which children had the lowest fevers. I gave each of them an assignment to help another child who was sicker than they. I got the children loaded in the carry-all and made them as comfortable as I could, making sure there were containers for vomit. Keith's parting words were,

"Now, don't let the engine die because it won't start. It is running off the generator."

I started out on the dirt road strewn with patches of ice and snow. I glanced down at my hands and noticed that the knuckles were white because I was gripping the steering wheel so hard! I was praying all the way that the vehicle would not die. I made it past Round Rock, so I knew I had gone about fifteen miles. Another few miles and I would be at Many Farms. I made it past there. Finally, I came to Chinle. Keith had called ahead and they had another vehicle waiting for me at the agency office. I transferred the children to the other van. As I drove on to the clinic, one of the children said, "Look, Mrs. Lamb, they just take she away!" I looked in the rearview window to see a tow truck pulling the carry-all down the street. (The children often got pronouns confused when learning English. "She" meant the vehicle.)

I got the children to the clinic, they got their medicine, and we headed home. It wasn't until I got back that Keith told me that he had called Round Rock and Many Farms and told them to watch for me to pass by. It would have eased my mind a great deal had I known that they were watching for me!

There were many other occasions when children had to be rushed to the hospital for appendectomies or other emergencies. We were told to take a child to the doctor if the temperature got to 101 degrees or higher. Our job was a 24/7 job. During the time we lived at the end of the dorm, it was not uncommon to have a knock on the door during the middle of the night. On one occasion, Keith had to take a little boy to Fort Defiance hospital for an appendectomy. We learned that if a child pulls his/her knees up and is complaining of pain in the abdomen, it is likely appendicitis. We also learned that Indian people have blood vessels closer to the surface of the skin in the nose. Nosebleeds were very common. Often, there would be a trail of blood droplets on the hall floor. Pillowcases were often stained. We taught the children that if the nose starts to bleed, pinch it and hold it for three minutes, then slowly let loose and don't touch it or bump it.

After our department head/guidance passed away, I moved back into my original office. For the most part, our duties went smoothly. There was seldom a runaway by now, and our main concern was supervising the aides. We had a small room where medical and first aid supplies were stored. Keith had one aide who kept drinking all of the cough medicine. We got cough medicine by the gallon, so he got quite a bit of alcohol from it. Some of my aids were very limited in the use of English, so, sometimes, it was difficult to get them to understand instructions. Sometimes they just "pulled high cheek bones." This was a phrase that meant that they played like "dumb Indian" and couldn't understand. We learned to tell when this was happening in most cases.

Keith and I took turns checking the night attendants. We tried to check at least one time each week unannounced. On one occasion, I found one of my night attendants in the boys' wing asleep on the lower end of a boy's bed while he had a thermometer in his mouth! I had suspected for some time that she would be having a hard time staying awake because we kept seeing her going here and there in the family's pickup during the day. I kept wondering when she was getting her sleep. We had received a number of complaints from the day aids that the work from the night before had not been done. It was obvious that she had been literally sleeping on the job.

I called her into the office and talked with her. "How would you feel," I asked, "if your children were in the dorm, and you trusted someone to watch after them at night and that person was sleeping and not watching your children?" I explained the danger of the thermometer in the mouth of the child should that child bite down on it. Since she was on a temporary appointment, I let her go. (It was almost impossible, to let someone go employed by the government once they had a regular appointment.) She got very upset with me and started spreading rumors around the community, and to the priest and nuns. I just held my grounds and tried to be nice. The worst part was that she was the wife of my interpreter and lived at the end of the dormitory. I hired another night attendant who knew that she had better not go to sleep on the job!

Several months later, the lady I had let go came sheepishly into my office and asked if she could talk to me. I welcomed her in. She said, "I know what you said was right. If it were my children, I would want someone watching them who would not go to sleep." She apologized. Of course, by now, much damage had been done in the community that could not be erased.

One of the things we tried to do with the children was to help them develop skills that would give self-confidence. The children, for the most part, were very shy. I decided to teach some of the girls how to twirl a baton. I ordered about ten batons, as I recall, and gave the girls lessons. We had a program in the dorm and all of my little girls marched in and did their routine. It was heartening to see the radiant looks of pride and confidence on their faces. They felt so very good about themselves because they were able to do something that not many people could do, and no one else they knew could do it.

A directive came from Washington, D.C. for us to test all of the children for physical fitness. We had a guideline of exercises to have the children do individually. Most of my little girls had a hard time sitting up when lying on the back. Other than that, they did fairly well. Most of the children, if not all, had herded sheep most of their lives and had much walking exercise.

One of our duties was to take inventory of supplies and do ordering. We had a set budget to use. Both Keith and I found that there were approximately 2,500–3,000 cans of scouring powder in each dorm. It seems that the people before us were trying to use all of the money in the budget and simply ordered scouring powder to use it up. The feeling was that if they didn't use all the money allotted, that next time the budget would be cut. Needless to say, we didn't order any more scouring powder. I am still wondering how many years it took to use up all of the scouring powder there!

A particular tough time occurred on a morning when some hesitant parents brought their little girl to the dorm. She was a year or two older than most first graders but had never been in school. She obviously was fighting coming. They brought her to me outside the dorm, and I understood that they were bringing her to school even though they could not speak English and my interpreter was not available at the moment. I took her hand, and she started fighting me. Finally, I picked her up to carry her inside. She kicked and cried. She pounded me with her fists and knocked my glasses off. I held on and took her into the dorm and turned her over to one of the aides to bathe and dress. The water in my eyes was for more than the physical abuse I had received. My heart went out to the children and parents. I knew it was really hard for them, but what was the alternative? The alternative would be for the child to continue sleeping on lice-infested sheepskins on a dirt floor in a hogan and never learn English or know any other life. The time would come when she would not be able to sustain life by herding sheep. Thankfully, she adjusted to school even before the black and blue spots on my shins, arms, and elsewhere had faded.

❧

We had somewhat of a unique staff, although perhaps not unique by comparison to other boarding schools on the reservation. It seemed that people came to work on the reservation for mainly two reasons. Either they came to genuinely help the Indian people, or they couldn't get a job anywhere else. Since not many people wanted to endure the isolation, jobs were almost always available on the reservation. Some of the employees were Indian and had preference over the hiring of Anglos. We were fairly well pleased with our dorm staff with the exceptional occasional problems, but I wondered about the school staff, particularly some of the teachers.

One time, we had two women teachers who came to work in a truck loaded with many things. In addition, they had a horse or two and some cows. It was a mother and daughter who had been hired to teach. The mother would say over and over, "Sugar is not as sweet as it used to be!" She went to great lengths to explain that she always ordered raw sugar. Some said that their apartment was filled with things piled up on top of each other. It was against the rules for people to bring livestock on the reservation, and the principal had quite a time convincing them that they couldn't have their livestock there. After the department head/academic caught the mother asleep lying on top of a table in the classroom while the children went unsupervised, they were finally let go.

There were a couple of black ladies on the teaching staff. One of them would sit and glare at me at baby showers that we had. She hardly ever talked, and she had a very scary glare. The other black lady did something that Keith and I still laugh about today.

One day, Keith got a call from the black lady just mentioned. She said that she had car trouble, and would Keith please come and get her. Keith immediately got in the car and went to help her. When he got there, she was sitting in the car smiling with her blouse off her shoulder and her bra strap showing. He fixed her car and came on back home. It wasn't long before he got another call that she was having car trouble again. Again he went to help her to find her smiling at him in the same way she was before. He again fixed her car and came home. It wasn't long before the phone rang again and she had the same story. He went to check on her and found that each time he went, she was a little further away from the campus. He finally concluded that she was leading him away from the campus for other reasons than fixing the car. He told her that he would not come to help her again, and came back home!

We had a black man who was a fine specimen of masculinity. He was good looking, very polite, and knowledgeable. On the first day of school, Keith had to discipline one of his boys for yelling out the window at this man. The boy was yelling *nakai-shinni* (my spelling) over and over. In English that meant "black

Mexican." It was a prejudicial derogatory term. I'm quite sure the teacher did not know what the term meant or perhaps didn't even know the child was yelling at him. We really liked this teacher. We invited him to our apartment to share Thanksgiving dinner. It seemed that everyone on campus liked him and soon he was dating the first grade teacher, a young vivacious lady who took a real interest in the children. They dated for some time and then she broke up with him. Apparently, he couldn't take the fact that she broke up with him. He started stalking her and causing her trouble. One night, we looked out our apartment window at the school and saw the lights on in the classroom of the young lady. She was working in the room, perhaps doing a bulletin board or other preparation for her class. I noticed a man looking in the window of the classroom. He would watch for a while, then walk around the school, then come back and watch some more. We told the principal, and I am not sure how he handled the situation.

This same man started making many trips to Gallup. It is tempting for most people to drive fast in the wide open spaces on the reservation when you can see for miles and see that no one else is on the road at the same time. This man, however, came closer to flying than driving. We were told that he was coming home from Gallup after we had experienced a hard rain. The ravine in the flats before the red clay hills by Round Rock had overflowed and washed out the bridge on the one road we had to use. He was going so fast that he didn't notice the bridge had washed out. Apparently, he flew over the ravine, and his car landed on the other side. Individuals on the staff were discussing what damage may have occurred to his car. He broke the front axle and the two front tires were pointed outward on each side. He didn't "fly" for a while!

When summer came, this man went back to Kansas, from where he had come. We heard that he ended up in jail. We knew nothing more about what happened to him. I felt sad. There was a stirring in my stomach as I thought about what might have been with this handsome, well-built, young man.

Other people on the staff included a Baptist family, a Mennonite family, and a sweet, dear, single Mennonite lady, Marie Kaufman. These were some of the people who had come to help the Indian people. Since we were all Christians, we met together for Bible study because the nearest Protestant church was fifty miles away. We took turns leading the study and hosting the study in our apartments. In addition, Miss Kaufman and I had Sunday school for the children of these families, and the children in one or two other families who came from time to time. We would have Sunday school at Miss Kaufman's apartment. Sunday school consisted of singing songs with the children, telling a Bible story, and doing a coloring activity. The priest did not like this and had people watching to make sure that none of the people he claimed for his church came to our Sunday school.

The Baptist family was there for the first year of our time at Lukachukai. It was the mother of this family who had come to the dorm waving the letter of commendation for her work with the hard-of-hearing boy who had changed so drastically after my long evening with him in my office. We never got to know them other than in the Bible studies we took turns hosting.

The Mennonite family makes us smile even today as we look back in our minds to our experiences there. The father walked with long, long steps, and waved his arms so far forward and backward that he reminded me of a windmill. He was a blustering kind of man with a tender heart but seemingly didn't think things through before acting. The whole family was very blonde. Being blonde or fair-skinned on the reservation definitely made one stand out with so many with black hair and dark skin. He was a teacher and his wife stayed home as a homemaker. They had three children, as I recall, and one of the little children informed me one time that her mom had said that she would have used that banana I threw away to make banana bread!

Our principal, Mr. Bearghost, was one of the very last Mandan Indians. Most of his tribe had been wiped out by smallpox when the white man carried the disease up the Mississippi River to his reservation in North Dakota. He told us that the old custom of his tribe was to select a gift for another very carefully. When giving a gift, one was to search his heart and decide what he had that meant the most to him. It was that thing that he liked the most that he was to give as a gift. When a young Mandan Indian man went deer hunting, he was to give the first deer he killed to someone else. He could keep the second deer he killed.

Mr. Bearghost's cousin came to visit him at our school. He gave Mr. Bearghost a portable air-conditioner for his car. (At that time, not everyone had air-conditioning in their cars.) The contraption sat in the front floor of the car between the driver and front-seat passenger. I, personally, never thought that it cooled the air very much; nevertheless, Mr. Bearghost was very proud of it, and he gave his cousin his best rifle in return.

On one occasion, the Mennonite family was preparing to go back to Kansas to visit their relatives there. The father asked Mr. Bearghost if he would like to have a gallon of honey brought back to him. Mr. Bearghost replied that he really didn't know what he would do with a gallon of honey and thanked him anyway. When the family returned from Kansas, Jake, the Mennonite father, went to Mr. Bearghost's house with a gallon of honey and charged him money for it!

This did not sit well with a man who had been taught to give what you like the most to another. He thought he might teach him a lesson when he got a chance.

The chance came one day when Jake knocked on his door and proudly showed him a Navajo rug he had purchased. Most of the non-Indian staffers prided themselves in the beautiful Navajo rugs they had purchased from the area natives. This was obviously a family that took pride in saving money. He had finally been able to afford a rug and was very proud of it and wanted all to see and know about it.

"Well, it *is* a pretty rug, but it looks like it has cotton warp threads in it and not real wool. But don't take my word for it.

Go, ask Keith what he thinks. He has bought several rugs and he knows."

Jake was devastated. He was crestfallen. He stood for a moment or two thinking and then said, "Well, I'll give it to my pastor back home. He won't know the difference!" You can imagine the opinion that Mr. Bearghost now had of this "fine Christian" who had been talking to him about Christianity!

I don't think that Keith had the faintest idea as to the warp threads of anything. I had learned in my textile class in college that the warp threads are supposed to be the strongest threads of the fabric and they run up and down. It really didn't matter, though, whether Keith knew the difference or not since they were playing a joke on the poor guy. As soon as he left our principal's house, Mr. Bearghost called Keith and told him what he had done and said, "He is going to ask you, so back me up on our opinion of the rug."

Sure enough, Jake came to our house to ask Keith; and sure enough, Keith backed up the principal's story. Of course, the Navajo people were much more likely to have wool from the sheep they herded than cotton. They spun their own thread from their wool. They had no cotton fields!

We never heard more about the rug, but I suspect somewhere in Kansas there is a proud pastor who owns a fine Navajo rug!

Mrs. Bearghost was a stay-at-home mom. They had one little girl who attended school with the other children. Mrs. Bearghost had much time on her hands and liked to spend a good portion of it at our apartment or house on my days off. She would come over, I would offer her coffee, and she would stay for hours. I couldn't get my housecleaning done or have any time to myself. She and Mr. Bearghost were of Catholic background but were not practicing their taught belief. Keith and I prayed about how to best witness and help them find a true relationship with Christ. Finally, after much prayer, I decided to tell Mrs. Bearghost how to be sure of this relationship. One morning, I got brave enough to talk to her about her condition. She got really upset with me. She stopped coming over. I had the satisfaction of knowing that at least she knew how to be saved, but I felt badly that she was upset.

Miss Kaufman was a dear Christian lady who became a close friend. We shared many concerns with her in our Sunday and Wednesday night Bible studies. When we had Bible study, she would always open her Bible and take out a neatly folded little white, thin, net cap, and put it on as she believed you were not to pray with your head uncovered. She was a lady who had a very regular routine. She got up at the same time each day, ate her meals at the same time each day, and went to bed at the same time each evening. She was of German descent and liked some of the foods common to many German people. She did not know how to drive and had no car! She would ride with the Bearghost's to Gallup, about 150 miles away, to buy groceries. She, the Bearghosts, and Keith and I did many things together. The Bearghosts never attended our Bible studies, but we prayed for them many times.

We were careful not to offend each other by our denominational views of the Bible. We each respected the views of the others. On one occasion, the discussion included the necessity, or lack thereof, of war. Of course, one of the basic Mennonite beliefs is that we do not fight. Mennonite men were conscientious objectors during WWII and were used for medical experiments. Miss Kaufman mentioned that she did not believe in fighting in war. Keith looked at her and said, "What if everyone felt that way?" She got a funny look on her face and said, "Well, if everyone felt that way, there would be no wars." Point well taken! I'm sure that Keith was referring to people in our country not wanting to go to war while others did. Then our country would be conquered.

Our Bible studies were very special to each of us. Many times, it was just Miss Kaufman, Keith, and I. The Baptist family left after the first year we were there. The Mennonite family joined us while they were there, but they, too, left the area before we did. We even took turns leading songs. It was our regular church time.

Mr. Bearghost was a very kind and intelligent man. He wore glasses and had a quizzical sparkle in his eyes. He liked a good practical joke as was evidenced by the Navajo rug incident. On one occasion, he took a gallon of pink water and a gallon of blue water to his agency meeting in Chinle. When he gave his report about Lukachukai, he displayed both and said that the main accomplishment on the campus was having babies. We had about five or six of our staff expecting at the same time. (I guess this was to be expected since we didn't have TV reception at that time and did not have movie theatres, etc., for entertainment!) We had a great deal of respect for him. He was soft-spoken and very perceptive. He had a deep understanding of the differences of the staff members, and he once said something that I have used over and over when talking to people about racial prejudice. He said that we should always think of people as individuals, not as a group. Although I think I had been doing that, I didn't realize until that time how many people do think of others in groups instead of individually. It is as though people expect all Navajos to be the same, all Hopis to be the same, etc.

Keith and I did learn a hard lesson from Mr. Bearghost. It was time for evaluation of employees. Mr. Bearghost asked each of us to evaluate ourselves. Keith and I were very honest and told areas where we thought we could improve. Mr. Bearghost gave us the exact evaluation we told him. At the same time, the maintenance man, cook, and others all received perfect ratings! We knew they were doing a poor job, but he had given them what they told him as well. We were rated lower than other employees!

Children did not stay in the dorms in the summer. During the time when they were gone, often the Bearghosts, Marie Kaufman, and Keith and I would do things together. On one occasion, we went hiking in Sheep Dip Canyon. This canyon is a tributary of Canyon de Chelly. We packed our lunches and headed out. We arrived at the top of the canyon where it wasn't so deep. Mr. Bearghost took a peek over the side and thought we could get down into the canyon at this point. He was just checking it out, but soon we were following. He later joked about helping Miss Kaufman down. She never wore slacks or jeans, but believed in wearing skirts or dresses only. Mr. Bearghost acted out how he would hold out his hand to help her as she slid down the side of the canyon, and turn his head sideways so he didn't see too much. It was his way of saying that he thought her belief of not wearing pants was silly. She always wore skirts that were full and loose fitting, so she could get around very well most of the time.

Soon, we were walking further and further into the canyon and realized that we had left our lunches in the car. After walking about two hours or so, we were famished! We came to a place where there was a little cave that we could get to on the side of the canyon. We found a couple of small pieces of rope that the Anasazi (ancient ones) had made from turkey feathers. There were lots of potsherds and a small pot. There were a couple of other items we found as well. Someone had been there before us. There was a small brown paper bag lying on the ground. Keith picked it up and found a can of Vienna sausages inside. We opened the can and divided the sausages among us. Few things have ever tasted as good as those sausages!

We decided it was time to head back to the car, so we turned and went back the way we came, following the canyon to the place we had first slid down an embankment to enter. The way back seemed much shorter than the trip there. There were some tired folks who went to bed that night!

We had several adventures on our days off. On another occasion, Keith and I decided to do some hiking by ourselves. We drove to Round Rock and just started walking. Soon we came up over a little knoll and lying before us was a field of smooth round rocks. We had never seen rocks like these before! We began to pick them up and look at them. For some strange reason, we had the urge to break one. Keith took one and pounded it against another rock until it broke open. The middle of the rock was a beautiful clear crystal! We couldn't believe our eyes. I'm sorry to say that we felt compelled to break a few more of the rocks to see if they were the same. Yes, they were all the same. There must have been hundreds of those rocks lying there. We left the spot and went back to campus to tell the Bearghosts and Miss Kaufman what we had found. It was a few months later that we went into a tourist gift shop at the Petrified Forest and saw similar rocks with insides of purple crystal and clear crystal. We found out that we had discovered geodes, semi-precious stones. We felt badly that we had broken some of them.

On another occasion, Keith and I went hiking alone on our day off and discovered a small cave on the side of a hill. We climbed the hill and went into the cave that was a little more than a shady spot under the outcropping of a rock. The ledge of rock jutting out had been important to someone. There propped up against the back wall were four rocks painted like masks. It was obvious that someone had meticulously painted them and that there was a significant meaning involved. Our first guess was that a medicine man had placed them there. This was one of the few times we had remembered to take a camera. Keith took some pictures and just as he was doing so, we heard a voice yelling at us. We turned around to see an elderly Navajo woman down below shouting something in Navajo. Although we could not distinguish her words, we had no trouble understanding that she was telling us to get out of there and leave things alone. We respected her wish! As we proceeded down the hill, she kept muttering something to us in Navajo. She was not happy with us! We were never able to find out what the masks were all about and our slides were destroyed in a flood in Montana a few years later.

Occasionally, we would decide to attend a squaw dance. Squaw dances were held late at night in differing locations. Information about them traveled by word of mouth, and occasionally, we would hear about one that was planned. We heard about one that was not too far from the school campus, so we decided to attend. I made some fry bread and coffee to take with us. (Fry bread is made by taking regular bread dough, rolling it very thin, and frying it in deep, very hot, fat. It puffs up and is hollow on the inside.

It is delicious with honey while it is hot. When it cools, it is nice to just sprinkle a little salt on it.) I put the fry bread in a brown paper bag. We had a thermos of coffee. We were prepared! We got in our old Dodge pickup and started up the road. Soon we found a group of folks gathered in an area. We parked our pickup and proceeded to go find a place to sit and watch. It was about seven o'clock in the evening as I recall. We kept waiting for the dance to start as we sat on the ground among the sagebrush, facing toward what appeared to be the center of attention. People were just milling around and talking. We kept wondering when the dance would start. Close to midnight our fry bread and coffee were consumed and we decided to give up and go home. No dance had started yet. We decided that they were probably waiting for us to leave before starting the dance. A few days later we heard that they had gone ahead and started the dance some time after we left.

At other times, we were able to see squaw dances and *yei-be-chi* dances as well. The squaw dances were just fun dances for the Navajo. They would simply dance around in a circle to the beat of the drum while some of the men would sing. I am convinced that there is no way to describe the sound of the men singing. To this day, when I hear similar drumbeats and singing on TV or elsewhere, I get chills and the hair stands up on my arms. The high, shrill, plaintive sound of the men singing sounds like a heartfelt, commentary on the situation of man. There is a depth of soul involved rarely witnessed by man.

This same sincerity is involved in the *yei-be-chi* dance. This dance is done in the fall after the first frost. It is a kind of harvest dance done in appreciation for crops raised. On one occasion, Keith and I sat on the steps of our apartment and listened to the chanting down the hill from the campus. We had a black Navajo rug hanging on the wall with the *yei-be-chi* figures in it. As they chanted, the moonlight shined through the window on that rug, and we could see it from the steps. We had an eerie feeling as we first looked at the moonlight shining on the rug and then cast our glance to the bonfire down below the campus and heard the "*Ooo-a-ooo*" of the men as they danced in a straight line back and forth. The leader of the line was the grandmother. Since the Navajo culture is a matriarchal society, the grandmother is the leader of the clan and has final say about decisions made. The men did the dancing, but the leader was called the grandmother. The last person in line was the clown. He did everything backwards. To the sound of giggles from the watchers, he would get out of line, go sideways or backward, and generally, do things differently from the others in the nine-man line. Those watching thought this to be very funny. All the men wore masks with strings coming down in front. As they went "*Ooo-a-ooo*," they would pull the strings. As Keith and I watched, we realized that we were part of very few white people ever allowed to witness such a sight. Although we certainly did not understand all that was happening, we could sense the sincerity being expressed by those involved and learned to appreciate the heartfelt appeal they seemed to be making to someone. I couldn't help but feel sad, however, knowing that so many people did not know about Jesus. In a community where the Catholic Church claimed that 98 percent were Catholic, it was especially strange to hear this type of worship taking place.

It was difficult to find good employees for the dormitory. We remembered a Navajo boy, Albert Footracer, who Keith had in his math class at Sanders. We contacted him to see if he would like a job as instructional aide. He took the job and lived with us since there were no available quarters. He was an exceptionally bright individual. When I was teaching at Sanders, he would come into my home economics room during lunch and fill the entire chalkboard with mirror writing. He would give a mischievous laugh and rewrite it the correct way. He had a real sense of humor, and he and Keith got along very well. Albert would go with us on our days off to various places.

Sometimes, we would go further away than the immediate area on our days off. The Hopi reservation is located in the middle of the Navajo reservation high on some *mesas*. It was said that the Hopis located there to be able to see the Navajo raiding bands coming from afar. In the old days, we were told, the Navajos would raid the Hopis and take some of them for slaves.

The Hopis had snake dances each August. We decided to attend one of these dances. The Hopi snake dance was publicized highly in the *Arizona Highways* magazine, and as a result, many people came from Phoenix and other places to watch the dance. Prior to the dance, the Hopi men would go up and down the mesas looking for rattlesnakes. They would catch them and use them in the dance. We got there on the day of the dance and did not see them gathering the snakes, but there was no doubt that there were snakes there. There was no place to sit. We all stood around trying to find shade under the overhangs of the pueblo buildings. The crowd kept getting bigger and bigger. Of course, the tourists did not know whether Albert, the Navajo boy living with us, was a Hopi Indian or not. Keith and Albert could not resist having a little fun. We were standing in the middle of a fairly large group of tourists who were all waiting for the dance to begin. "Albert," Keith said, "is it true that when they get through with the dance, they throw the snakes into the crowd?" Albert caught on to the joke right away and with a straight face answered, "Yes, they always do that." Of course, Albert had no idea what took place. He had never seen a snake dance before. They continued making up things and talking back and forth. You could tell that the crowd was listening to every word they said and the crowd began to back up away from the area where the dance was to take place. I could hardly keep a straight face. Keith and Albert were having a great time. We were able to see the happenings of the dance very well since the crowd had backed away! I'm not sure what the tourists thought at the end of the dance when the snakes were taken down the hill and turned loose.

It was nice having Albert stay with us. He and Keith decided to do mountain climbing at Round Rock. I was afraid they would really get hurt. They got up quite a way and decided to come down. I was relieved. Neither of them knew what they were doing.

Albert was good with the children. He spoke both Navajo and English and was very intelligent. He was a hard worker. It was clear that he was able to do more than as an aide. After he left us, we heard later that he had become a policeman in Los Angeles. I have no doubt that he was a good one. We wanted the best for him. He had come from a home with an alcoholic mother. Our little church at Sanders had taken food to the family but always broke the bread loaves and flour so the mother could not sell them for money for alcohol. I had taught his sister in home economics. She had a fiery temper! She was one of the few Navajo children who could cause a little discipline problem.

One time each month on our days off, we would make a trip to Gallup to buy groceries. I had Tuesdays and Wednesdays off; Keith had Wednesdays and Thursdays off. I would clean the house thoroughly on Tuesday. When Keith got off work on Tuesday, we would head for Gallup and get there in the evening. We usually stayed at the El Rancho Motel. We would do our shopping on Wednesday morning and head back to Lukachukai on Wednesday afternoon to enable me to be at work on Thursday.

The El Rancho Motel was special to us. Many movie stars had stayed there while filming Westerns in the area. The rooms were named for the stars who had stayed there. Of course, John Wayne had stayed there as had several other popular Western stars of the '50s. They had a beauty salon there and I could get my hair fixed. The food was good as was the service. After a restful night, we would do our shopping. We bought our dairy products at a dairy where they would pack them in dry ice for the trip back to the reservation. The other groceries we bought at Jay's Supermarket. A real treat for us was to order a pizza at Jay's as the last item on our list. We would eat it in the car on the way back home. To this day, we have never found pizza as good as Jay's pizza!

If the weather and roads were good, we would take the car to town. If they were not good, we would take the truck. It was standard procedure for us that when we got stuck in the sand or mud, Keith would get out and push and I would slip over behind the steering wheel to drive. I didn't know until we lived on the reservation that vehicles could get stuck in the sand. It would seem to shake the vehicle to pieces as we would try to move on.

On one trip to Gallup, we kept getting stuck in the mud. Our pickup was covered with mud. We were so embarrassed that we parked in the back of El Rancho and went in the back door so no one could see the truck. We didn't look too good ourselves. We were really embarrassed and glad to get a bath that night.

We decided that it would be really helpful to have a freezer. Since we had to purchase a month's supply of groceries at a time, we needed a way to keep them. We bought an upright freezer, tied it in the back of the pickup, and started home. It had been drizzling rain most of the day, and the red clay hills were "as slick as snot" as Keith put it. We started up the hill, slipping and sliding all the way, sometimes coming dangerously close to the steep edge. We were inching our way along and the truck was about to stop and go backward. I climbed out the side door and climbed up over into the back of the truck and positioned myself over the rear axle. I began jumping up and down to give the truck traction. It worked! I jumped up and down until we got to the top of the hill and then I got back into the front of the truck. I was wet and tired. We got the freezer home, but the next day, I was sick with strep throat. The doctor wasn't due to come to the campus for several days. I was running a high fever. Someone went to the Catholic mission and got the nuns. They came and gave me sulfa. It seemed strange to have the nuns in their black habits walking around our apartment! The next day, I had big red bumps all over my back. The nuns came back and told me it was a reaction to the sulfa and that I should drink a lot of water. That was not a pleasant time!

On our way to Gallup one day, we stopped at Many Farms to buy gas. Keith went inside to pay for the gas, and I thought he would never come out. I kept looking to see if he was coming and every time I would look, I noticed that the men inside the station were looking at me! I was puzzled. I looked down at myself to see if something was wrong with me. Perhaps I was not fully dressed? Finally, after what seemed like an eternity, Keith came out with a big smile on his face. He got in the car, started the engine, and said, "You know, those men wouldn't believe that you are a hillbilly! I told them that you are from the Ozarks and that I bought you your first pair of shoes! They said that they didn't think that you looked like a hillbilly!" I was so mad at him!

Winters at Lukachukai could be vicious! We were about nine thousand feet altitude as I recall. During one bad storm, Keith had gone out to help folks, and I was in our apartment worrying about him. We had about nine inches of snow and it was still coming down heavily! Suddenly there was a loud knock on the door. It was unusual to ever have a knock at the door as we hardly ever had visitors that far up on the reservation. I hesitantly went to the door. When I opened it, there stood two total strangers, each with a small book in his hand. One of the men said, "Pardone me…How you say?…We are hopelessly lost!" He was looking at his little book as he was talking. They had French-English dictionaries and could speak only a little English.

There I stood, a young woman alone in an apartment, with two Frenchmen at my door deep in the Navajo reservation! The snow showed no signs of letting up. I was wishing Keith were there. Then, one of the men suddenly remembered and reached in his coat to bring out a note. "Pat," it said, "put these men up. They are lost." It was signed by Keith.

Now this was a dilemma. How was I going to take care of two Frenchmen who couldn't speak English. I couldn't speak French. Besides that, I wasn't sure it was safe to have them there. I had to wonder a little about my husband telling me to put up two strange Frenchmen! What was I to do? I couldn't turn them out in the snowstorm. There were no motels within miles and miles. I'm not even sure there were any motels on the reservation at that time. I invited them in. Through their broken English I learned that they had worked in the oil fields in French Algeria and saved enough money to come to America to see "real, live Indians." They had seen Western movies and wanted to see Indians for themselves. I don't know how they made it as far as they did in the big Chrysler New Yorker on the snow covered dirt roads.

Since we could not communicate, I decided to get out the slide projector and show them some of the pictures we had taken. This worked well. They especially enjoyed seeing pictures of the reservation. At one point they both got excited and said, "Stop, stop!" Again in broken English they were able to communicate to me that the hieroglyphics on the wall in one of the slides was just like what they had seen in French Algeria. It was interesting to the three of us to know of the similarity.

Finally, Keith came home and all was well. I cooked for them all, and we put them up for the night. The next day, they went on their way. We never heard from them again.

One bad storm came right at Christmas one year, and our three-times-a-week mail did not get through. My family in Missouri was always so good about sending gifts! We made the mistake of counting on those gifts and had gone ahead and given our personal gifts to each other early thinking we would have the ones from home to open. When Christmas morning came, we sat looking at each other with no gifts to open. I think that was the loneliest Christmas I can remember. We learned a good lesson though. We had each other, and we were both in good health. The material things were not so important. Anyway, we had something to look forward to when the storm finally cleared and we got the packages from Missouri.

Sometimes, the Navajo parents would take the wheels off their wagons and put sled runners on them to come and pick up their children when we had the snowstorms. I was excited to get to ride in one such "wagon sled." It was fun, although, I got out of bed to do it. I had strep throat. It seemed that I had a lot of tonsillitis and strep throat while there. I finally decided that I was catching it from the children when I would give them hugs. At the age of twenty-six, I went to Ganado Presbyterian Mission and had a tonsillectomy. After that, I just got ear infections and bronchitis!

When the children made get-well cards for me, I noticed that almost every card had mirror writing. As an educator, that was very interesting to me. We hear so much about dyslexia and special teaching methods for it. I remembered when Albert, the young man who had lived with us used to do mirror writing on my chalkboard in the home economics room and then turn it around. He was a very intelligent young man. I have wondered through the years if the much adieu about dyslexia is really warranted. Could it be that it is simply a matter of being able to read and write either way and that possibly those people are actually more intelligent in that respect? Maybe, it is like people who can use the right hand and left hand equally. I now suggest that possibility to my GED (General Education Diploma) students when I teach. It seems to encourage them.

We were living on the reservation at the time when the Navajo people had just begun accepting the white man's ways. Since electricity had not yet come to the reservation, other than generator-powered electricity on the government school campuses, there had not been much exposure to the outside world. Most of the old traditions were still honored. The young people, as so often is the case, were beginning to change a little. On one occasion, a young girl came to me and asked if I would bake a wedding cake for her wedding. I had never decorated a wedding cake before, so I asked for help from the wife of the new trader at the trading post. She and her husband had recently come to run the trading post. She had decorated wedding cakes before and gave me her recipe for icing and some tips on decorating. The next time we went to Gallup, I bought a cake decorating set and some little silver edible BBs dragees. They looked like little BB's. I made the cake all white with simple designs around the edges and put a little silver BB dragee in the middle of each little flower. Actually, it wasn't too bad for my first try! She had this cake along with the traditional Navajo wedding cake at her wedding.

The traditional wedding cake was baked in the ground. A hole would be dug in the ground and a fire built in it to heat it as hot as possible. The fire would be removed and the hole would be lined with corn husks. Corn meal (blue, yellow, or white) and raisins would be placed in the hole and enough water to make the cornmeal like mush. The cornmeal would have been ground on a grinding stone. The hole would be covered and the cake left to bake overnight. I was given some to taste and did not enjoy it. The ashes that somehow managed to get mixed in the cake somewhat distracted from any flavor there might have been. I'm sure there was some dirt mixed in as well. I could understand why that tradition was not cherished!

Medicine men or relatives usually conducted the weddings for the young brides and grooms. The wedding party had certain directions to observe when seated for the ceremony. In many of the Navajo ceremonies, attention was given to the four directions. The medicine man would indicate north, south, east, and west. East was the most important. (Hogans were always built facing the east.) There was always a washing of hands of both the bride and groom before the wedding cake was eaten. This was to indicate the cleansing of the body, mind, and spirit. Part of the ceremony included putting some of the wedding cake (traditional) in the middle of a wedding basket and the medicine man sprinkling pollen over it in all four directions. He would sprinkle from east to west, then from south to north. Then he would make a circle in the center of the basket to represent the sun. This was to unite the couple in the Navajo universe. It indicated planting seeds of life as they would bring new life into the world when they became parents. The bride and groom each ate some of the cake with their hands.

There were basic components of the weddings, but some variations often occurred. Sometimes, there would be a speaker who gave advice. The older people of both families would often give advice. The medicine man sometimes would say something like the following, in the Navajo language:

> Now, you have lit a fire and that fire should not go out. The two of you now have a fire that represents love, understanding, and a philosophy of life. It will give you heat, food, warmth, and happiness. The new fire represents a new beginning—a new life and a new family. The fire should keep burning; you should stay together. You have lit the fire for life, until old age separates you.

At one time in the history of the Navajo tradition, a new hogan would have been built for the new couple to live in. I expect whether or not that was done depended greatly on the resources of the couple's families.

It is interesting that the divorce process is much simpler than the wedding process. The Navajo society was matriarchal and if a woman wanted a divorce all she had to do was put the husband's saddle outside the door of the hogan. If he came home and found it there, he knew he had been divorced! There is no way to verify this, but this is what we were told.

There were a few horses around the area. One of the instructional aides brought his horse for me to ride. It was in the evening and was just dark enough not to be able to see well, but there was enough light that you thought you could see well enough. Since the horse was not shod, I was running him along the side of the road in the grass so it would be softer on his feet. We were running along when I looked down and saw a big loop of steel cable sticking up out of the ground. It was too late to do anything about it. The horse got his left front leg caught in it and went down. I went flying over the head of the horse. My glasses ended up several feet away from me. I looked up to see blood coming out of the mouth of the horse. His tongue was cut almost all the way across. I just knew that the horse had also broken his leg. I called for Keith to come and help.

As it turned out, I was unhurt except for some soreness from the jolt of hitting the ground, but the horse had a difficult situation to deal with. He did not break his leg, but his tongue was in bad shape. His owner called a medicine man to sing over him. On occasion, the owner would inform Keith that he needed some money for this or that for the horse. This went on for several weeks. Finally, Keith stopped the money and the horse got better.

It was embarrassing to find out later that most of the children in Keith's dorm had been watching and saw me take the spill. "Look! Mrs. Lamb, she just fall!" They exclaimed with noses pressed to the large windows, so we were told. We found out later that when the dormitories were built, the trash was covered with dirt. The cable loop that was buried in concrete had been exposed over time from rain.

There were lots of little sidewinder rattlesnakes around the campus. They are just as poisonous and bad as the big rattlesnakes. On one occasion, a rattlesnake was on the step right by the door of my dormitory, when the children started to go to the dining room. The Navajo belief was to take the snake away and let it go to its own home instead of killing it. One of the aides was able to get the snake away. On another occasion, Keith and I were walking down the road from our Bible study that we held at Marie Kaufman's apartment. There was not very much light. Our campus did not have street lights. I thought I saw a piece of string that Keith was about to step on. Suddenly, it moved! He almost stepped on the snake. That one got killed!

A Navajo lady worked for me one day each week to clean the apartment and do the ironing. (We still ironed things then!) It was nice to have the help. One Sunday afternoon, her husband came to visit us. He sat and visited for a long time, before he finally got to the reason he came. It was tiring for us to be patient and wait for the Indian folks to get to their point. It seemed to be the custom to visit for a long time before we could ever find out the purpose of the visit. Finally, he said, "You have something." The three words didn't tell us very much. We thought, "Yes, we have some things." He repeated, "You have something." We didn't know what he was talking about. Finally Keith said, "What do you mean?" It turned out that his wife had seen somethings while working for us that Keith and the boys at the dorm had found on a hike.

Keith often took the boys on hikes. They had found some things that a medicine man had left in a field. Keith had picked them up and brought them home, not realizing their significance to the Navajo people. They had found a small bunch of weeds grouped together with fiber from a plant that looked like a rubber band wrapped around the bottom of the bunch of seeded grass or weeds. There was down of birds tucked in the top of the bunch of grass. In addition, there were three circles of twigs, about three inches in diameter, held together by the same substance as the bunch of grass. They had been very carefully placed. One was directly above the bunch of grass and one was on either side.

"If you don't put the things back where you found them, you will get a headache or backache, or something bad may happen to you." The husband of my helper was very serious as he spoke. It was obvious to see that he was quite concerned. He went on to explain that the medicine man had placed the objects there in a certain direction to make the illness of a person leave that person and go in another direction. If we didn't put the objects back, he thought the illness would come in our direction and make us sick.

One Sunday afternoon, Keith had a group of boys up in the nearby mountain when one of the boys said, "Mr. Lamb, what time is it?" Keith, feeling like a real Indian looked at the sun said, "It's about two o'clock." "We're supposed to be in church!" they said. Keith had not seen the memo about the special church activity. They ran all the way back to the school and down to the Catholic mission. They were late!

The priest was not happy. He filed a complaint with the principal and also the office in Gallup, N.M. Keith spent several months trying to defend himself for not having the boys in church. There were several hearings. The situation was never fully resolved. Keith had found the memo in the trash after the hike and has always suspected that a particular aide had thrown it away intentionally to get him in trouble. Needless to say, the priest was always watching us to find something wrong in what we did. He did not like it because some of the staff met in our homes for Bible study nor that the Mennonite lady and I had Sunday school for children of the staff in our homes. The situation was such that it was impossible to do our jobs as we thought we should in good conscience.

Keith applied for a job in Flandreau, S.D. and was accepted. Since no "little lambs" had come along by this time, we decided that I would not work and we would start our family. We began making arrangements to move.

It was another cold, winter day in January when the moving van arrived. Although the sun was shining and it looked warm outside, it was several degrees below zero, as I recall. When the movers opened our door to load the few things we had accumulated, the plant across the room turned black. Keith was working outside on a vehicle at the time the movers were loading and froze the edges of his ears. It didn't take a long time to load the few belongings we had and we were soon on our way.

We felt very sad to close this chapter in our lives.

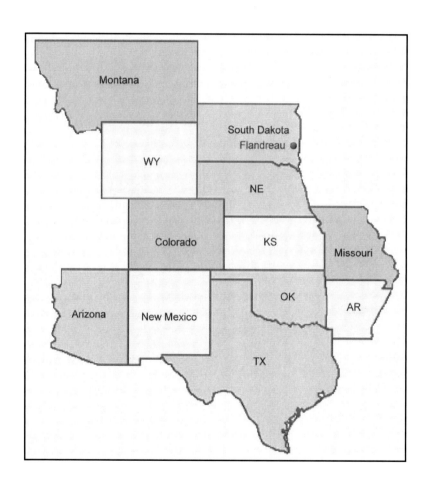

A Test of Endurance

Flandreau, South Dakota

*B*efore moving, we had made a last trip to see our friends at the children's home in Chambers. We didn't feel we would need the pickup back in South Dakota, so we gave it to Lael and Elbert, knowing they could make good use of it. We gave it innocently enough with good intentions. We learned later that the mission headquarters thought that the truck should be theirs. Not only that, Keith's folks in Nebraska were upset. His mom said, "Your dad could have used that truck!" Seems that sometimes, good intentions don't always turn out with good results. Elbert became somewhat disillusioned with the idea that the headquarters in Flagstaff would want the truck. I don't know if that had anything to do with their decision to leave Chambers and move back to Tennessee. We learned that Lael and Elbert later had two biological sons. That may have influenced their decision. We had little contact with them until several years later.

Flandreau was like a different world. We were back in green country! There were trees and rivers! Flandreau reminded me of my home in Missouri. Even though we arrived in January in the cold of winter, there was still a feeling of the Midwest that was welcome to both Keith and I. We had loved the Southwest, but we had been long enough away from the Midwest, where we both were raised, that we had begun to miss it.

The government boarding school was across the river from the small town of Flandreau. One got the feeling that it had been planned that way on purpose to keep a divide between the Indian people and those living in the small town. In order for the students to get to town, they had to cross the bridge. It wasn't long before Keith found out that one of the most important duties expected of him was to serve as "the mean old troll" on that bridge to keep the students from going to town.

We were once again living on the end of the dormitory. Flandreau had two dorms, one for girls and one for boys. We were now with high school students. Most of these students would tell us that the judge had told them they could either go to a reform school or to Flandreau. This told us immediately that most of the kids had been in trouble. They came from several states and represented several different Indian tribes. It was sad that many Indian children, not only at Flandreau, but on many reservations throughout the country had problems. I'm certain that there was a real difficulty in trying to please parents and tribal leaders on the one hand who were telling them to stay with the old Indian ways, and the white man on the other hand telling them to learn the ways that would help them succeed in life. In addition, it was not easy to be taken away from home and familiar surroundings. There were many of the children who were able to deal with it acceptably, but many could not. The confusion often surfaced in negative ways. The boys at Flandreau were battling many conflicts inside themselves.

Soon after we moved in, I received a visit from the town's welcome wagon one day while Keith was on duty. Three ladies came to visit and gave me a few coupons to use to shop downtown. They talked for some time about how it was difficult to get the merchants to cooperate and give coupons. They really didn't want to do it because so many of the government workers from the school stayed for such a short time that the merchants felt they didn't get their money back from any shopping they might do. When they left, I really didn't feel that I had been welcomed, but rather had been told that I should be sure and spend more money in town than I was getting in gifts!

Keith quickly learned that the reason he had been selected over others for the job was his size and background. He had the body of a football player and looked big and strong. This was a necessity for survival at this school. Shortly after we arrived, there was an incident where the students hid behind a door on second floor of the dorm and called for an instructional aide to come to the room. Upon his arrival, they rushed him, picked him up, and threw him out the window. He spent several days in the hospital with broken ribs, etc.

Our time at Flandreau was very difficult for Keith. He felt that he could not really help the kids because he had to "play policeman" all the time. I'm sure that to this day he has not told me everything that happened. He did not want to worry me. It was surely a test of endurance for him.

On the other hand, I felt that even though I was not employed by the school, I was able to counsel and help several students. Since we lived at the end of the dorm, I had easy access to the students. They would often come to the apartment for popcorn, cookies, etc. The church we chose was in Pipestone, Minnesota, about fifteen miles away just across the state line. I was able to take several of the boys to church and some of them accepted Christ. Since Keith had to work most Sundays, I often took the boys by myself. A very nice Christian farm family took a special liking to the boys and would often invite them to their home for dinner on Sundays and take them back to church on Sunday nights. This was such a wonderful thing! It meant so much to the boys.

One boy who liked to visit our apartment was the son of a golden gloves champion. He was known as the fighter of the dorm. I would never have known this if Keith had not told me because when he came to see me each afternoon after school, he would tell me about finding a pheasant's nest, how many eggs it had, etc. He and I took that mama pheasant all the way through hatching, and I heard about the babies! He seemed so innocent and childlike to me. He was always very polite.

One time, this young man told me in detail how he had gotten in trouble. He and some others had robbed a filling station in Wyoming. He told me that he and some friends were drinking. They were just driving around. They noticed they were almost out of gas. They stopped at the filling station to get gas, but it was closed. They got mad because they couldn't get any gas so they decided to break in, get the key to the pump, and fill up their car. They broke the window and when they got in they saw all the candy, pop, etc. They began to help themselves. Then they saw the safe. They couldn't get it open so they decided to take it with them. They got their gas, loaded the safe, and went up into the mountains. Somehow they managed to get the safe open. I don't recall that he told me how they got caught.

This young man was a perfect gentleman to me. I took him and some of the other boys fishing in the nearby river often. We would take the fish home and fry them. At least, I was keeping these guys occupied and out of trouble. I never had any trouble with any of the boys. They seemed to respect me. I didn't know until after we left Flandreau that they were probably even protecting me. Keith had talked to some of them and they were watching out for me.

It was fairly common at each government school to receive visitors from Washington, D.C. Sometimes, congressmen or people from the Bureau of Indian Affairs came. On one such occasion, Keith brought a gentleman down to the apartment and introduced him. Trying to be hospitable, I offered him something to drink. He sure had a funny look on his face when I handed him Kool-Aid! We never had alcoholic beverages in our home and on the spur of the moment, it didn't occur to me that he was expecting something else.

Keith and I had often talked of adopting Indian children even if we were to have our own biological children. I suppose our friends at the Children's Home near Sanders had influenced our thinking. We felt that God wanted us to work with the Indian people. Watching our friends with foster children who had come to them with problems made us think that it would be much better to adopt a baby and start working with the children when very young. We had been married four years by now and it seemed time to start a family if we were ever going to do so. We inquired and found that there was an office of Lutheran Social Services in Sioux Falls, South Dakota. We decided to go through the process of adoption.

We went through several counseling sessions with the people there. On one occasion, the lady asked Keith a question that should have been answered no. She worded it, "You wouldn't do _____ would you?" "Yes," he said. She looked at him so strangely! We had a problem. On the Navajo reservation, all the children would answer a double negative question with "yes" meaning "Yes, I would not do that." Keith had picked this habit up from the children. It took him some months to get over it. After explaining the problem, the lady seemed to understand.

The agency required that I see a doctor before we adopt to determine why I had not become pregnant. When we did so, he told me about a procedure that was being tried whereby a small wedge would be cut out of one ovary to stimulate ovulation. He wanted to know if I would be willing to have that procedure done. I told him no. I explained that my sister had been married four years before she got pregnant and that I felt that if God wanted me to get pregnant, I would without the surgical procedure. He told the social worker that he would not recommend us to be good parents because I did not want a child bad enough to go through the procedure. I was pretty upset. I explained my thinking to the social worker and she agreed with me. Of course, we also told her that we felt that God wanted us to adopt an Indian child.

After a few weeks, one day we received a phone call from the social worker. She had twin girls ready to be adopted and wondered if we would be interested. I relayed the information to Keith and he was noncommittal. I thought I would wait for his decision. Nothing happened.

A week or so later, we received another call from the social worker. She now had a little boy ready to be adopted. He had been sick with pneumonia and they had been afraid he might die, so she had not told us about him. When I told Keith, he said, "It would be nice to have a little boy around the house." We said yes.

Kenneth was two months and three weeks old. We were given very good instructions for his care. We picked him up in the morning, and that afternoon, the church we had been attending gave us a baby shower. I put him in the church nursery upstairs and the shower was downstairs in the basement. During the shower, he began to cry. One of the ladies went up to get him. He would not stop crying. She handed him to me and immediately he stopped crying and relaxed in my arms. The ladies remarked about how he seemed to already know his mother.

Kenneth was raised by the book as far as his physical care was concerned. His food was measured exactly and he was on schedule. He was a good baby. He got a bath at the same time each day. The boys in the dorm loved to help me take care of him. On one occasion, we took him with us fishing. When it started to sprinkle, one of the boys (the same boy who had been part of robbing a filling station) picked him up in his infant seat and ran to the car with him, so he wouldn't get wet. It was hard for me to believe that some of these boys had been in so much trouble because they acted so nicely around me.

We were pleasantly surprised to find that there was a golf course on the school property. It was right behind the apartment.

Keith and I have never called ourselves golfers but we availed ourselves of the opportunity. We would take Kenneth with us in his infant seat, set him down at a safe distance, and then carry him from hole to hole. It was nice to get some fresh air during the summer evenings. Kenneth seemed to enjoy it, too.

We had very little opportunity for recreation other than the golf. However, there was a ping-pong table in the basement of the dorm, and sometimes, we would go downstairs and play. Keith's hours at work were scheduled for when the students were not in class. During the day, we had the basement pretty much to ourselves. As soon as the boys came back from class, Keith had to go to work and worked well into the night or even morning hours.

Pipestone was named for the Pipestone National Monument located there. This was where the Indian people had quarried their stone to make peace pipes in days gone by. As most national monuments are set up, this, too, had the little printed guides where tourists could stop at numbered locations in the park and read information from the brochure. My sister, Wanda, and brother-in-law, Snags, came to visit us and we took them to the park. As we walked along from numbered point to numbered point, Snags would read the comments from the brochure. We began to notice that the other tourists had begun listening to us and were not bothering to read their information for themselves. Snags could not resist the temptation to have some fun. He began to embellish the comments. I noticed that his voice kept getting louder and more and more expression was in his reading. Soon, he was like a guide giving a lecture. When we came to the final point, he said, "Here, ladies and gentlemen, is where Hiawatha jumped off a cliff because she was so heartbroken over her lover." Keith, Wanda, and I could hardly keep a straight face. I'm not sure if the tourists ever caught on that he was making up most of the things he was saying. Of course, Hiawatha was no place near Pipestone.

We were not at Flandreau very long. In fact, as I recall, it was less than a year. Keith put in for a promotion and transfer. He was chosen to be in charge of a boys' dorm at Cutbank Boarding School near Browning, Montana.

We hired a moving van, packed a camp cook set and a few necessities to last until our other belongings arrived. We saw that the van was loaded. We left for Montana.

Looking back now, it seems that God just sent us there to adopt our first son, Kenneth. Kenneth was Cheyenne River Sioux. At the time of this writing, he is now grown and the program director for AIDS awareness for Native Americans and is working with seven tribes in the Northwest. His office is in Bellingham, Washington.

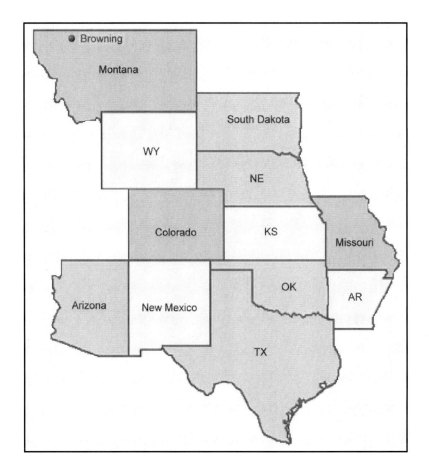

The Big Flood

Browning, Montana

Outbank Boarding School was actually outside of Browning, Montana, about thirteen miles east. It was a picturesque setting. It sat on the bank of the Cutbank River at the bottom of a steep hill. The campus consisted of a few old brick buildings, log houses for quarters for the government workers, and two sprawling dormitories that had been built more recently than the other buildings. The dormitories were built of concrete block whereas the older buildings were built of brick or logs. The brick buildings housed the administration offices and the kitchen. Everything except the dormitories was quite old. The years of bad winters had taken their toll in spite of obvious efforts to keep all in good repair. Glacier National Park was a few miles west of Browning. The Canadian border was just to the north of us.

I had always wondered what it would be like to live in a log cabin. I was about to find out. Our cabin backed up to the river. That was nice. Someone had planted horseradish in the backyard and it had liked that spot very much. It grew over an area of about twenty feet in diameter. A picket fence enclosed the frontyard. That would prove convenient for letting Kenneth play outside during the few times when it was warm enough. The cabin, itself, had two bedrooms, a living room, kitchen, and unfinished basement. There was a front door and a side door. The side door opened to a small landing where one could choose to go up about five steps to the upstairs or ten or so steps to the basement. I was glad to see a door was at the top of the stairs that I could keep closed to prevent Kenneth from falling down the stairs. The heat was provided by an old furnace that heated water to run through radiators upstairs. It proved to be a nice, even heat for which we would be quite thankful during the many subzero days and nights to follow.

The inside of the cabin needed painting badly. We hurried to get the painting done before the furniture arrived. The hurrying was unnecessary, as it turned out, because our furniture did not arrive for about three weeks. We found that as soon as we left Flandreau, the moving company had subcontracted to another company because they had gotten a big contract with Boeing in Wichita. In the meantime, we slept on sleeping bags on the floor and I cooked with a camp cook set. We had bought several pieces of ranch oak furniture while in Flandreau and we were missing it at that time.

Finally, the furniture arrived and we settled in. We found a church about fifteen miles away. The pastor was Dick Raweater, a Blood Indian from Canada. We grew to love Dick very much. He lived in a small house, typical of the Indian homes in the area, near the church. Since there was no piano player, I was asked to play the piano. I also taught the small children in Sunday school. It was a two-room church. The main room where the preaching was held had a wood stove for heat. There was another wood stove in the other room where fellowships were held. That was also where I taught my Sunday school class. This was a Baptist church whose headquarters were in Ohio.

When we moved to Browning in the fall, we found that it was already cold there. During that first winter, we would go to church with snow on our boots and leave with the same snow still on the toe of our boots. During the week, Dick would go along the small stream that ran behind the church and pick up twigs or fallen branches to burn in the wood stove. Our heat depended on how much wood he was able to find. When I played the piano, my hands were stiff and cold. I would rub my hands between songs to warm my fingers to play.

Keith decided to take a leadership role. "Dick," he said, "let's get some people together and take a Saturday to go cut some wood, so we will have some on hand and you won't have to go gather some each week." There was one other family in the church other than Dick's relatives, so we didn't have a lot of people to help get the wood. Keith rented a chainsaw, and he and two other men went up into the nearby mountains one Saturday and cut wood. The church was a little warmer for our services after they were able to get more wood. However, the area to heat was much too big for the one wood stove and it was still not really comfortable. We had bought some soft leather boots for Kenneth. He would chew on the boots and they would freeze. He wasn't walking yet, so we had to hold him all the time.

When summer came, Keith suggested they go cut wood in the summer so they would have wood for the next winter and be better prepared. He didn't much like the idea of waiting until it was so cold to go cut the wood. He once again organized the guys, and they went up into the mountains to cut wood for the following winter. They came to a place where there were large stumps standing about twenty feet high. "Who in the world just cut the tops out of those trees and left such big stumps?" Keith asked. The other guys laughed at him. "We did!" they said. "That's where we cut wood last winter!" Keith was sure surprised to find that the snow had been so deep when they cut the wood. He thought they had cut the trees off at the ground. Nevertheless; now they had trees with no branches which made woodcutting this time a little easier.

It seemed to us that Dick had such a pure, clean heart. Since he did not have a job other than the pastoring of the small church, he depended on Social Services for support of his family. He would pay for his own gas from his welfare check to go visit and witness to folks. He would put tracts in boxes of clothing at the thrift shops. On one occasion, he, Keith, and "Red," the father of the other family who attended, went to Canada and stood on the street corners and handed out tracts. It was quite an experience for Keith to visit Dick's reservation and friends.

Dick's preaching touched us deeply. He said, "People ask me why I preach. They say I am poor, and I should just quit preaching. I tell them that I am not poor. My father owns the cattle on a thousand hills. I am his son. I am rich." On another occasion, Dick said, "My children complain about not having enough to eat. I tell them, 'Don't complain. You get one hot meal a day a school. Your mother and I don't get that.'" We felt good about tithing at this church.

Keith found his work much easier in Browning than it had been in Flandreau. He was in charge of the boys' dormitory that housed elementary school children. The bus from the public school in Browning came and picked them up to take them to school at the public school. The children were mostly Blackfeet Indian. They came from very poor, and often very dirty, homes. Keith always had a way of bonding with the children and here, as at Lukachukai, he planned many outdoor activities such a hiking, camping out, etc. There were horses available for the children to ride, and I took advantage of this opportunity.

One day, Keith told the boys to saddle me a horse. He stayed home to take care of Kenneth, and I went to ride. I trustingly got on the horse but couldn't get it to do anything. It just stayed in the corral. I gave up and went back home. Keith asked me which horse I rode and I described it for him. He left the house and I didn't know until years later what he had done. The boys had saddled a horse for me that had never been ridden. He found out who had come up with the idea and made that boy ride the horse. They made the horse leave the corral, and it really bucked with him. I guess he had quite a ride! Keith told the boys, "Don't you ever do that to my wife again!"

In Browning, as had been the case in Lukachukai, our chief recreation was hiking. Keith had a big windbreaker jacket, and he would put Kenneth on his stomach and snap him inside his jacket. Off we would go through the woods. We have always been nature lovers. There were so many beautiful birds in Montana. There were warblers of so many different colors and red-winged blackbirds were profuse. Through the church, we became acquainted with a large family who lived in Cutbank, MT, a few miles away. Del and Goldie Wahl owned a large wheat farm not too far from the school. Sometimes, we would go over to their farm and ride their beautiful palomino horse. On one occasion, I was riding the horse and racing the car that Keith and our friend was in. I really liked that horse!

The children in the dorms were allowed to go home on weekends. Keith remembers with tears in his eyes about one little boy who went home for the weekend and didn't come back. They checked the school to see if he had gone directly to school rather than coming to the dormitory. He was not in school. Keith got in the government car and went to his home. There he found a really nasty place. There had been an egg fight, and eggs were all over the beds, furniture, walls, and even the ceiling. The bed had no sheets and the mattress was so dirty he could not even see the stripes in the ticking that covered it. An old man was drunk and had passed out with vomit on his face and running down his neck. The little boy was on the dirty bed and had a really high fever. Keith carried him to the car and took him to the public health hospital. He had pneumonia. After a few days, the hospital personnel called the school and said he was ready to be released. Keith went and got him. Keith asked him why he would go to that place when he had clean clothes and a clean bed at the dorm. Keith said, "Here you have horses to ride and you can run in the woods and play. Why would you want to go there?" The little boy looked at Keith and said, "That's my home."

The winters were long. It was so cold much of the time. I bought myself a *Learn How to Knit and Crochet Book* and taught myself to knit. I knitted a sweater for Kenneth and a cap for Keith. Since I loved to sew, we bought a brand new sewing machine, and I spent a lot of time sewing. Occasionally, we would drive up to Alberta, Canada, and I would enjoy looking in the fabric shops. They had beautiful wool fabrics. I bought some wool and made matching sport coats for Keith and Kenneth. The principal asked me if I would be a Girl Scout leader, and I agreed to do it if the girls could come to our house rather than me having to take Kenneth out in the cold. Almost every weeknight, except Wednesday when we went to church, I would have a few girls over for Scouting. They worked on and earned several badges. They enjoyed using Kenneth for their child care badge activities. We gave a program for the rest of the children. The Girl Scout song was, "Hail to Sacajawea" which was so appropriate since Sacajawea was an Indian woman who served as guide for Lewis and Clark when they explored their way to Montana.

The dormitories were connected with one huge recreation room. The principal decided to order new furniture for the room. There were several chairs, couches and tables. One day, Keith called me and said that the principal wanted me to come over and arrange the furniture. I have no clue as to why he chose me to do this. When I got there, several of the staff members were standing around looking a little scared. The principal was a man who liked to use a lot of profanity and did not hesitate to let his feelings be known. It seems that several of them had tried to make suggestions as to how the furniture needed to be arranged, and he was displeased with their ideas. I did not know what they had suggested. I was standing there looking at the furniture for the first time with a crowd waiting to see what would happen. With

Kenneth on my hip, and a lot of silent prayers going up, I started looking at the unfamiliar furniture and room. I ventured a comment. "We need conversation and reading areas," I said. "Well, where do you want us to put this couch?" the principal asked. I made a quick count in my mind of the number of chairs, etc. Slowly, I began to tell them where to put things. With the final comment, "You will probably move everything as soon as I leave." I left and went back home. Much to my surprise, they never changed the furniture. The Lord sure helped me with that one!

One very cold winter night, our furnace decided to stop working. It was several degrees below zero. No one on campus offered to house us. We called our friends in Cutbank, and they immediately invited us over. I bundled up Kenneth as much as I could. We got in the Volkswagen van that we had bought and made into a camper, turned on the heater, turned on the supplementary heater we had installed for the camper, and Keith placed a small portable heater in the front with us. We were still cold as we went to their home. We stayed with them a few nights until our furnace could be fixed. How nice it is to have good friends!

One weekend in early June, it rained and rained and rained. The winters there were long and there was much snow up on the mountains. The snow began melting rapidly due to the rain. We woke up on Monday morning with the rain still coming down. Keith went to work as usual, but this was to be a very unusual day. He soon came back to the house and asked me to help him put air in our small rubber raft. They needed it because it had rained so much that some people were being flooded out of their homes down the valley from the school, and they were going to try to go get them out of their homes. About an hour or so later, he called to tell me to get ready to leave the house that he was going to come after Kenneth and me. By this time, the river behind the house was out of its banks. It was almost to our back door. I threw together a few things. My mind was whirling. What do you take in an emergency like this? I grabbed a bottle of Clorox because I knew we would need to use it to have water to drink since all water would be contaminated. I grabbed a jar of peanut butter and all the jars of baby food we had for Kenneth. I got all of his clean diapers and put all of the tea towels with them in case I ran out of diapers and would have to use them. (We didn't have disposable diapers available then.) While waiting for Keith, I went downstairs and saw that water was coming in the basement fast. I quickly grabbed a bucket and began baling out the water. Silly me! I was pouring it in the utility sink and it was coming back up the drain in the floor! I grabbed all the meat from the upright freezer and carried it upstairs and put it in the refrigerator. I used the wire basket from the freezer to hold the things I decided to take with us. I placed the vacuum cleaner and everything I could from the floor on a table. Finally Keith came in a flat bed truck. He had someone take our Volkswagon camper out to the hill going up the road from the school. He went next door and got the father of the lady who was in charge of the girls' dorm and helped him on the back of the truck. By this time, the water was rising very fast. It was rushing in our side door. As I walked out, carrying Kenneth, the water was rushing in the side door and I waded in knee deep water in our own house! Keith carried the wire basket of items I had put together. Kenneth and I sat in the front of the truck with Keith. As we drove through the water, I was thinking of my new sewing machine. "Well," I told Keith, "The Lord giveth and the Lord taketh away. We are young. We can start again." We realized that we might lose everything that was in that house.

Keith left Kenneth and me with the Volkswagen on the side of the hill. I put Kenneth in the back of the camper and stood outside watching the entire valley fill with water. Water was swirling around all the buildings. I still remember Kenneth's little nose pressed against the back window of the Volkswagen watching through the glass. Others were there also. Everyone on campus had to leave their homes. By now, the rubber raft was useless. The water was very swift. The principal managed to get a small boat from someone, and he, Keith, and some others were still trying to get downstream to get people out of the way of the rising water. They decided to tie ropes to the boat and the men would hold the ropes to keep the boat from getting away from them. They tied a rope to each end and it began to spin like a top. The man inside the boat fell out and was washed up against a barbed wire fence at the side of the road. They got him back to safety and decided that they needed three ropes, using one on the side to keep the boat upright.

All day, the men worked and worked trying to save as many people as they could. Radio reports began to come in. There was one horrifying story after another. One lady was floating down the river on a log with her baby. Helicopters had come to help. The pilot of one helicopter spotted her and flew close to her. She tried desperately to lift her baby up for them to get. She dropped her baby in the water, never to see it again.

A priest climbed a tree and waited for several hours before a helicopter picked him up. One man and woman cut a hole in the roof of their house and took turns watching for the helicopter to come as their house floated down the river. Finally, the helicopter spotted the man and picked him up. When he was safely on the shore, he said, "By the way, my wife is in the house, too."

The lady who lived next door to us was trying desperately to load her valuables in her car to get them to safety. She put her silver, fur coat, and many other things that she considered precious in her car. The men went to get her to safety but she wouldn't come because she kept making more and more trips back to her house for more and more things. Finally, the principal used some of his familiar profanity and told her to come on. As she started to get in her car, the men, using all their might, could not hold onto it in the strong current. It went floating downstream with all of her valuables in it. She, however, had not yet gotten in the car and managed to get to safety.

During the day, somehow, we managed to find the time to go over to the church and get the pastor's family. The church was on a small stream that had become a river. Two girls with small babies came with us, but Dick and his wife remained to watch after the church. I confess that I was exasperated with the girls. They each had on coats and sat with their babies with no blankets on them. Finally, I could stand it now longer. I said, "Girls, if you have to wear a coat, don't you think your babies might be cold?" Then they wrapped up their babies.

Several cars, people, and homes had been washed away. When the men had done all they could, Keith, Kenneth, and I went to Browning to get something to eat. When we came back, after dark, the National Guard had arrived and some of the guards were guarding the school. They were not going to let us go there because they were guarding against looting. Before Keith could convince them that we belonged there, one guard actually cocked his gun at us. He finally let us through. The water had subsided enough that we could get to the large brick building that housed the dining room and offices. Several of the employees spent the night in that building as did we. It was not a comfortable feeling to hear the water swirling outside around the old foundation. We were wondering if that old foundation would crumble. I went into the office and pushed two leather chairs that had side arms together to make a bed for Kenneth. I had just gotten him asleep when a lady came running downstairs screaming, "The dam broke! The dam broke! They just said it on the radio!" Of course, she woke him up and I had to start to comfort him all over again. She was so panicky. Almost everyone seemed really frightened, but she was the worst. I learned that at times like that, it doesn't help anyone to get so upset. None of us got much sleep that night.

The next day, public health people arrived to give us shots. We had to have gamma globulin shots to boost our immunity. They brought a pair of scales and each of us had to step on them before getting our shot since the dosage was determined by our weight. Everyone was somber and tired. One by one we dragged ourselves to the front of the line and stepped on the scales. When it was Keith's turn, he gave a huge sigh and said, "Oh! I'm clear up to 180 pounds!" Everyone laughed because it was obvious that he hadn't been as low as 180 pounds for a long, long time!

After two nights in the large brick building in the center of the campus, the water had subsided enough that we could go back to our house. Talk about a mess! Thankfully, the water had not gotten upstairs, but it covered our upright freezer in the basement. There was fine mud silt all over the basement. The smell was not good. We had a lot of cleaning to do!

Keith took the freezer apart and spread the insulation in the front yard to dry. All it needed was a new fan since the motor was sealed. The fan cost $15. He put it back together and we used that freezer for about sixteen more years! (We highly recommend General Electric freezers!) The timer on the washer did not work, but the dryer was operable. I could still use the washer by turning the timer manually. I would put a load of clothes in, let them wash, run upstairs to work, then run downstairs to turn the knob to spin, then run upstairs again to work, then downstairs to turn the knob to rinse, etc. I'm sure Kenneth had the cleanest diapers in the world. Sometimes, they would wash or rinse a long time before I would run downstairs to turn the knob.

During the flood, the table I had loaded with things from the floor, floated. Nothing on it was harmed. I had left the slide projector and some slides on a top shelf. Some of the slides were ruined. We were very grateful to our Lord that we had been so protected. We couldn't help but think of our next door neighbor who had lost all of her valuables trying to save them. I think there is a lesson here.

For a few days after the subsiding of the water, Keith drove a bus of prisoners down to different areas to look for bodies. He was with them when one body was found. He later took me there to show the place. He said, "Where you are standing was not here before the flood. You are standing on trees that were washed downstream and piled on each other." Dirt filled in between the trees. A schoolhouse had washed away, also, and he said it might be beneath us. I don't know if all the bodies were ever found. The last count we heard was ninety people who lost their lives in that flood. Recently, I checked the Internet about the flood and found that a sculpture of old cars ruined in that flood is outside of Browning.

The flood happened in June. We were still waiting for summer in August, when the first snowflakes fell. It was time to start thinking of staying inside again. This winter, we would be preparing for another baby. We had decided to adopt another child. We contacted Lutheran Social Services again and got the ball rolling.

We had to make several trips to Great Falls for conferences with a psychologist. We were required to read four books about adoption. Finally, the day came when we were to go pick up our new baby! We named him David Lee. Kenneth had Keith's middle name, O'Neil, and we would give David my middle name, Lee. He was a good baby as Kenneth had been. It was obvious from the start that he did not like vegetables. I tried to give him some squash and he spit it out at me. He was three months and one week old when we got him. The adoption agency required a dedication service for all of the adoptees. We heartily agreed even though it included sprinkling for baptism. We believe that a person must be old enough to be responsible for a decision to live for Christ before being baptized. "It's just a little water on the head, we thought. It doesn't hurt anything." In the ceremony, we had to promise to teach David the Ten Commandments. That was fine with us. We were quite pleased with the processes we went through with Lutheran Social Services for adopting the boys.

After the dedication ceremony, we drove over to see our Mennonite friend we had worked with at Lukachukai. Marie was now working in Busby, Montana, near the Custer Battlefield. We spent the night with her. Keith sat back in her recliner when we got there and put David on his tummy. They both went to sleep in the recliner. We still have a picture of that scene! We did have one unfortunate incident when Kenneth bit David's foot while I was changing David's diaper. David had on stretch terrycloth sleepers with the feet in them. There were little white fluffy balls on the feet of the sleeper. The white ball was wet from Kenneth's saliva. To this day, I don't know if Kenneth bit him on purpose or if he was just biting the fluffy ball. I had really worked hard to get Kenneth to accept a new baby in the home. Maybe it worked or maybe it didn't!

We kept busy that winter with the two boys, church, Scouts, and Keith's work. Keith was hungry for a promotion. He had been given several responsibilities such as acting principal, etc., but there had been no increase in pay. We now had an additional mouth to feed. He put in for a transfer to Point Barrow, Alaska. He had it all figured out. There was nothing to spend money on there and government workers got paid extra money because it was so isolated. He thought we could go there and work and save our money, then come back and buy a farm. He did not get the job. Instead, he put in for a job as principal at Ramah Dormitory in Ramah, New Mexico, and did get that job. We rented a U-Haul truck, packed it ourselves, towed the Volkswagen, and headed for New Mexico.

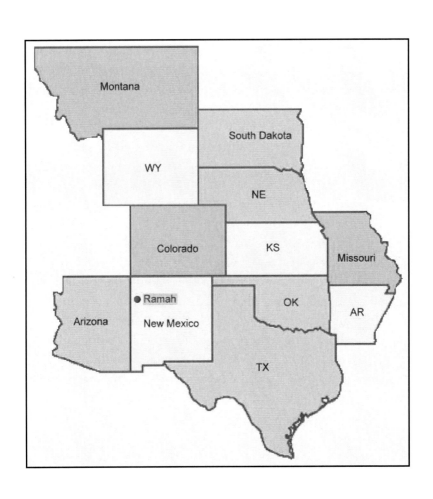

The Big Snowstorm

Ramah, New Mexico

The actual physical move to Ramah was the best we had made so far. Kenneth sat between Keith and me most of the way, and Dave was on my lap. (Car seats were not required in those days.) We packed and loaded everything ourselves. We left on time and arrived on time with nothing broken.

We gradually left the green of Montana and entered the desert-like country of the Southwest. Since we had lived in Sanders before, it was almost like going back home. Sanders was forty miles west of Gallup and Ramah was approximately forty miles south of Gallup. Zuni, New Mexico, was twenty miles west of Ramah.

It felt good to be back in Navajo country! Although we would be located in what is known as the checkerboard area, we would still be working with Navajo people again. The checkerboard area is actually south of the big Navajo reservation. It is the area where ranches of the white man are dispersed throughout the area, a ranch here and there and reservation in between the ranches.

When we saw a Navajo man walking beside the road, we knew we were almost there. His familiar characteristic limp, seen in a large number of the Navajo people, reminded us of the congenital hip problem many of them had inherited. We had been told that it shows up every fourth generation and is somehow connected with the story in the Bible of Jacob wrestling with the angel when the socket of his hip was touched and he was made lame. I do not understand how this could be true, but that is what we were told.

Finally, we topped a hill and started down the long sloping highway to a valley where a large cluster of cottonwood trees was visible. There were a few houses scattered here and there on each side of the road. As we neared the cluster of trees, we realized we had reached Ramah.

We passed a small restaurant and a filling station. We turned on a dirt road and drove under the huge cottonwood trees we had seen in the distance. It was a community of small houses with no paved roads. The campus of the government boarding school sat up above the high school. (We immediately noticed that the high school was badly in need of a face lift and repair.) We crossed a cattle guard as we entered the campus and found the office. Keith left us in the truck and went to find someone in charge. He found his new boss, a fairly young and confident man, who took us to our new home.

Our house was made of concrete blocks that had been painted an adobe color. It was built on a concrete slab and had dark brown speckled tile on a concrete floor. (I mopped and waxed those floors many times!) It had two bedrooms, a bath, a kitchen, living room, and dining area. It was just a few steps from one of the two dormitories. It was adequate and very typical of government quarters. We often joked that you could walk into any government quarters blindfolded and go directly to each room. They were pretty much alike.

The campus consisted of two dormitories, an office, and some government quarters, all built of concrete block painted an adobe color. All of the buildings looked as though they had been built in the early sixties so they were not old. David celebrated his first birthday here and he was born in 1965. Navajo children came in from the reservation and stayed in the dormitories while they attended public school. Keith's job was to see that the children were cared for properly. He supervised the dormitory personnel and coordinated activities between the government dormitories and the public school.

Ramah was a unique place. It was a small Mormon town that had been settled in the days of the "wild" West. I can't remember who told us that it was a town of Jack Mormons. This term apparently meant that the people there had drifted away from the strong beliefs of the church and deviated somewhat from its rules. It was rumored that the trader sold tobacco under the counter, for instance, in spite of the fact that Mormons as a group were known not to use tobacco. The huge cottonwood trees gave away the age of the community. We were later told that the settlers brought the startings for the trees in a wagon and planted them on arrival.

As we became more acquainted with the community, I remember being surprised to see so many houses in the little community unfinished. We were told that the residents would live in the houses while building them to save money. It was apparent that some folks had been living in those houses for years and still had not finished them. Some houses had dirt floors but the walls, roof, and remainder of the house looked finished or near finished. The people were friendly and welcomed us. It soon became evident that there was a real concern in the community about keeping their high school open. It was about to be condemned. The community hated to see it go and was struggling to find ways to keep it open. This fact was to later affect my daily schedule.

The early settlers had built a dam up the valley on one side to create Ramah Lake for irrigation purposes for their gardens or more industrious ventures. There was a group of graves by the lake.

There was an interesting story connected with the graves by the lake. We were told that the graves were of some pioneers who came through the area in a covered wagon in the old days and discovered an abandoned cabin where the family spent the night. Little did they know that someone had died from smallpox in that cabin. The entire family got sick with smallpox and died. When I heard this story, I understood why God commanded Moses in the book of Leviticus to burn down the house of people who died. I remembered, too, that the old Navajo custom was to burn a hogan when someone died in it. Now, this made sense.

The campus of the school where Keith was to be principal was located a few yards from the old, run-down, high school building on one side, and the newer concrete block public elementary school on another side. The Navajo children came in from the reservation in the fall to live in the two dormitories and attend the public schools. There was one individual who supervised Keith when we first arrived. After a short time, he transferred to another area and Keith was promoted to the position vacated, making Keith entirely responsible for the campus. When Keith was promoted, we moved to the house next door which was built the same, except for a third bedroom, but was a little better situated for privacy in that it was exactly at the mouth of the little box canyon. We liked this house better because we could have horses. We bought Smoky and Rex and we would often go riding in the evenings.

A dirt path ran from the campus of the dorms to the Nazarene Mission up the hill beyond the public elementary school. Most of the Navajo children who lived in the dorm were Nazarene. The Mormon folks had done very little to win the Navajo to their church and didn't seem to mind that the children all went to the Nazarene mission each Sunday. Mrs. Blanche Byrd was the missionary there.

Mrs. Byrd was a very active and strong leader. Her husband was mild-mannered and talked very little. He did the maintenance around the mission. She had done an outstanding work there. They had a teenage daughter who was afflicted with arthritis. There was no doubt as to who was in control of the work. It took very little time for her to ask Keith and me to teach Sunday school classes. We agreed. She went to Albuquerque to the Baptist Book Store and got the flannel graph materials for us to use. Each Sunday, we dressed Kenneth and David, took them to Sunday school with us, and taught two classes. Mrs. Byrd insisted that they had prayed the other principal away and that God had sent Keith.

We were amazed at how strong in their faith the Navajo people were. Every Sunday, they came to the mission in their pickup trucks loaded with people. Mrs. Byrd told us that they tithed from their welfare checks. It was not unusual for some of the people to go to homes of individuals and pray for them. We were told that an all-night prayer meeting was held in a hogan of a man who had been drinking alcohol a great deal.

⚬

It wasn't long after we moved to Ramah that I was approached by a Navajo gentleman from Window Rock, the capital of the reservation, and asked to direct a Navajo preschool near the chapter house on the reservation. This was approximately thirteen miles from our house. I accepted the position and worked with two instructional aides who were to prepare lunch for the children and assist as needed in cleaning, etc. They could speak English but preferred to speak Navajo. This meant that I was the only fluent English speaker within several miles. It got a little lonely at times. I learned enough words to know when they were talking about me and that, at times, was discomfiting.

A Navajo gentleman was paid to drive and interpret for me as I went to the hogans on the reservation to recruit children for the school. We went in his pickup to the places where he thought there might be children the right age to attend the preschool. Most of the people were receptive. I remember visiting a hogan on one occasion where an elderly Navajo lady was squatted by her fire outside. She had a large cast iron skillet on the fire filled with grease. She was making fried bread. Ordinarily, I love fry bread, but as I watched her make the bread, I noticed that quite often she would wipe the water off her face that was running down from her eyes. Her eyes were filled with white soft matter. She looked up at me with a big grin on her weathered and wrinkled face and said, "Yahteh." After I responded, she continued talking to me. The interpreter explained that she was offering me some fry bread. Now what was I to do? I wanted her grandchildren to come to school, so I didn't dare offend her. However, I knew that many of the Navajo people suffered from glaucoma, an eye disease. The interpreter was watching me to see what I would do. Was this white woman going to insult his people? No, she wasn't! I smiled, took the fry bread and said *"Akaha"* (a-ka-ha) which means "thank you" in Navajo. *"Nshone,"* I said. *Nshone* (n-sho-ne) means "good." She gave me a big toothless grin. We signed up three children there as I recall.

In the fall, many of the Navajo children eat a lot of corn and melons. As many people know, corn does not digest well with younger children. There is a tendency for the children to get diarrhea. I remember an incident while I was teaching in the preschool when a little girl had a problem while we were in group time learning English names of objects. I began to smell a terrible odor. We discovered that the corn she had eaten did not digest well. I asked the instructional aides to take her and clean her up, so I could continue with the other children in their learning session. They began talking to each other in Navajo and then to me. They refused to clean her up. They didn't want to be bothered with such a terrible task. I took the little girl to the bathroom, helped her off with her panties, and had to wash them in the sink and clean her up. It was not fun! I've thought many times since about some churches that practice foot washing to show humility. I laugh when I think about how they announce it ahead of time and everyone washes their feet before coming to church. I've thought to myself that perhaps the chore I did may have shown a little more humility.

As director of the preschool, I was required to attend a workshop. I couldn't believe my ears when I heard that the workshop was to be at Lukachukai, the very same place where Keith and I had worked before. I would be sleeping in one of the very dorms that we had once supervised.

The workshop was conducted by persons from the University of Arizona, in Tempe. I don't remember a great deal about what was taught, but I vividly remember an incident that occurred one night while we were there. One of my instructional aides was pregnant, and she hadn't told me. After the lights had gone off, someone came to me and told me that my instructional aid was sick. I got up, went to check on her and found that she had had a miscarriage. The nearest hospital was in Fort Defiance, near Window Rock, more than sixty miles away on a dirt road. The fetus was about six to eight inches as I recall, and had a head and other recognizable features. We got a towel, placed the fetus in the towel and wrapped it up. We put the instructional aid in the backseat of my car and we started to Fort Defiance. The road was bumpy, and I did the best I could to drive so as not to cause more pain. When we got there, she was examined and released. The doctors were glad to get the fetus for a specimen and were going to put it in formaldehyde in a jar on a shelf where there were several others.

I went home over the weekend knowing that I would need to come back for another week of training. Keith took me back the next week and made arrangements for a Baptist missionary from Zuni Pueblo to use his plane and come and pick me up at the end of the week. We had met this missionary and driven over to Zuni from Ramah to attend the mission. We were looking forward to seeing the area from the air. Finally, the workshop was over, and they were there to pick me up. Keith had brought Kenneth and David with them. I was so glad to see them!

We got in the plane and took off. Things were fine for awhile. Then, our pilot, the missionary, decided to hotdog a bit. We were going over Canyon de Chelly. He made a dive down and said, "Do you want to see it a little closer?" Before we could answer, we were circling and diving, and getting sicker and sicker. I began to lose my food. I looked at Kenneth and Dave to see how they were taking it. Kenneth, three years old at the time, was looking at us with disgust. He was not a bit sick, but Mom and Dad were having a rough time. David seemed to do all right as well. We were glad when we finally got home!

One thing that I have always felt badly about is the fact that David, at the age of thirteen months, took his first step while I was at this workshop! Nothing can ever make up for the fact that mommy was not there to see that first step!

It wasn't long before the principal of the public elementary school in Ramah approached me about taking a job teaching kindergarten. I kept telling him that I wasn't interested because I was teaching out on the reservation. He kept after me until I finally gave in. I had not been under contract to direct the preschool and there was a question of funding to continue the project. It was not the custom to sign contracts for such jobs. Driving the thirteen miles back and forth was not much fun and to teach at the public school would give me more time with the boys. They also wanted me to teach home economics at the high school to help them be accredited and save the school. I taught kindergarten at the elementary school, used my lunch hour to teach a home economics class at the high school, then back to the elementary school for the rest of the day to teach kindergarten again. I was a good customer for Slim Fast as that was what I had for lunch each day.

I had a very nice instructional aid at the elementary school. My aide was artistically inclined and did all the bulletin boards, cleaned the room, helped the children put toys away, etc. I could go ahead and have group time while she was helping the stragglers get to the group. Teaching kindergarten there was extremely enjoyable and rewarding. Although I did not have an elementary certificate, my instincts seemed to lead me to do the right things. I was on a temporary certificate and had to take correspondence courses to become fully qualified. My students were half Anglo and half Navajo. Some of my Navajo students knew no English at all, so it was a real challenge to teach English speaking and non-English speaking students at the same time. Thankfully, we had a principal who gave the teachers some latitude in using instincts. The teacher across the hall and I became very good friends. She taught pre-first. (Pre-first was a class of non-English speaking six-year-olds who went into her class to learn English before going on to first grade.) We worked out our own team teaching. At a certain time each day, she would take my non-English speaking five-year-old children and work with them, and I would take her children that she thought were ready to read and I would work with them. By the end of the year, ten of my kindergartners were reading as were some of the children she had sent to me.

Most of the training we received there came from UCLA. We were told not to try to teach reading until the children could speak English. Fortunately, I wasn't told this early enough because I began to teach the sounds of the alphabet and use old primer readers with the children right away. I got scolded severely by one of the instructors from UCLA for teaching reading. Her theory was that reading should not be taught until the children could speak fluent English. My feeling was that a great deal of English was not needed to read, "See, Dick" or "See Dick run." To me, they could learn both at the same time. Later, I was so glad that I did what I did when I could see the looks of pride on the faces of my little ones for being able to read. During rest time, I allowed children to take books and look at them. Toward the end of the year, some of the children at various times would pop up off their mat and exclaim loudly, "Teacher, I can read!"

At the end of the next year, a teacher went to the principal and said, "Why don't you put Pat in one of the upper grades, and let that teacher we have who just likes to play teach the kindergarten." I agreed to take second grade. I got the same students I had taught in kindergarten. At the end of the year, the class as a whole tested on fourth grade level in spelling. One of my little non-English speakers liked to read so much that he always hurried through his math to read a library book. He kept a book on the corner of his desk all the time. His older brother, in sixth grade, could not read as well. The principal approached me and asked me to tutor his older brother and the older brother of one of the other non-English speaking students I had taught in kindergarten. The two younger brothers had big smiles on their faces when their big brothers came into the room to learn to read. (The big brothers had been taught the UCLA way.)

My instructional aid had a beautiful wedding. She had a beautiful white wedding gown and was married in the Nazarene mission. It was a melding of the old and new. Most guests came in traditional velvet, squaw skirts, and turquoise jewelry. It was a beautiful ceremony.

About a year after they were married, they had the cutest little boy, and she always dressed him so neatly. It was so sad when the baby got a severe case of diarrhea. Nothing seemed to work for it. The public health doctors even contacted doctors in Brazil because they thought it was a kind of diarrhea experienced there. Nothing worked, however, and the little baby just wasted away. The father and mother grieved deeply. On top of this, the father's brother had been killed in Vietnam. He would sit and play tapes of his brother talking over and over. He got in a state of depression from which he never recovered. He told our Navajo policeman, Chimeco Eriacho, that he was going to get drunk and have a wreck and commit suicide. Chimeco kept a close eye on him as much as possible. About 3 a.m. one morning, Keith got a call from the Navajo policeman. There had been a wreck, and he wanted Keith to go with him. They found the pickup wrecked and my aide's husband with his head buried about six inches into the ground. He had kept his word.

The husband was Mormon. The funeral was to be in the Mormon church. My aide asked me to give the invocation. How was I ever going to do it? I've never been to a funeral in my life without crying. As for that matter, I had never been in a Mormon church before. This took some serious prayer time before the time of the prayer!

The day came for the funeral. The church was packed. The casket was open in front of the pulpit. For some strange reason, I wasn't crying. (Not so strange, actually. It definitely was an answer to my prayers.) It came time for the invocation. I did it with no trembling voice or tears. I don't remember what I prayed, but I felt so good knowing that God had given me strength.

The winters could be vicious at Ramah. Just a few miles down the road was the continental divide so our altitude was pretty high. I'll never forget the terrible snowstorm in the late sixties.

It had snowed and snowed all weekend. We were fairly safe right on campus, but we began to worry about the Navajo people out on the reservation in their hogans. Ranchers, too, had to be worried about their cattle. The snow was at least two feet deep on campus, and drifts where the wind was blowing strongly were sometimes over the head.

When it didn't stop snowing by Monday morning, Keith decided he should find a way to go check on some of the people on the reservation. He knew most of the families and knew which ones were most likely to be in need of help. Since the roads were impassable, he decided he should probably get a Ski-Doo. He and some of the other staff were able to go a little ways by truck on the main road, so they hauled the Ski-Doo in the truck as far as it would go and then unloaded it for Keith to take off.

He didn't realize that Ski-Doos were not as safe as they appeared on TV. This particular one turned out to be very undependable. The snow would clog up the track and it would stall. He was on his way to the Garcias' home when, sure enough, it stalled for good. Up to this point he had been able to dig the snow out of the track and get it to go again.

When he had started out that morning, I suggested he take matches with him. I always accused him of thinking he was superman and not being as cautious about things as perhaps he should be. "Oh," he said, "I won't need those." I shoved them into the pocket of his hooded sweatshirt even though he didn't think he would need them. It was a good thing that I did.

He was a long way from any hogan and all he could see were the tops of pinion trees sticking out of the snow. He dug himself a hole in the snow, tore off part of his T-shirt, soaked it in gasoline from the skidoo, and started a fire by pulling some bark off of a downed tree and finding a dry spot. He warmed himself by the fire and tried to decide what to do. He knew that soon it would begin getting dark.

Pretty soon, he heard a cow moo. Knowing that there was a rancher who had a ranch in this checkerboard area, he decided that the cow must be close to a barn or shed. He wondered if he should try to go toward the cow. What if he started that way and the cow stopped mooing? Then he would be out in the middle of nowhere and possibly freeze to death. He listened and heard the cow moo again. He opted to follow the sound of the cow.

The snow was so deep that it was exhausting to walk through it. He had to stop often and rest and listen for the cow. She faithfully kept mooing. By now, it was getting dark. He knew he had to keep going, or he would freeze to death. After walking for what seemed an eternity, he found himself falling down between hard things. He couldn't figure out what was happening. He only knew that he had to keep going. He would step on something hard, then take another step and fall down. He wondered how long he could keep this up. Apparently, he was walking on farm machinery that was covered with snow. Then, he saw a light. He decided to go toward the light. Closer and closer he got and finally realized that the light was in the rancher's house. The snow was so deep that he hardly knew when he stepped on the porch. He finally came to the door of the house and knocked. The rancher opened the door and he practically fell inside. The rancher gave him some coffee and food and let him stay the night.

In the meantime, back on campus, I was worried silly because Keith hadn't come home. I had received a phone call or two during the day from some of the staff who had come over to Ramah from Zuni. Each time, they were assuring me that Keith was all right. I thought it strange that they were reassuring me so early in the day. I had not yet even questioned whether he was all right. However, I did wonder why there were so many men in his office. Later, I began to get worried, and I decided I would bake some cookies and take them down to them knowing they were all tired. By going down to the office, I might find out more about what was going on.

I bundled up, got the plate of cookies, and headed out. When I opened the office door, there stood four or five men with strange looks on their faces. They definitely looked surprised to see me. They thanked me for the cookies and told me not to worry about Keith because, "We all know that he knows the reservation like the back of his hand." I could tell that they didn't want me hanging around, so I left and went back to the house.

After I got back to the house, I got a call from Ed Hodge, the Department Head of Academics. He and Keith had become close friends. He leveled with me and told me that they didn't know where Keith was. He explained that Keith had taken off and was supposed to meet them at a certain time but did not show up. They had called Albuquerque to get more Ski-Doos to go look for him. Someone brought the Ski-Doos but did not bring the keys to start them!

It was a sleepless night. Finally, I got a call about 3 a.m. the next morning telling me that they had found Keith. Ed had called the McKinley county sheriff and gotten him to bring a weasel. He and the sheriff had gone out together on the weasel to follow his tracks. They were able to locate him.

Keith told me when he got home that as they returned past where he had built the fire, there were tracks all around the tree where the guys had kicked the snow looking for his body. They thought he had frozen.

I've always said that if I could find the cow that kept mooing, I would put a big ribbon around her neck!

Keith had no time to rest from his ordeal. Needs still had to be met. Connections had been made to bring in the National Guard to help. The day he got home, he found that there were plans to send tanks, trucks, and a helicopter along with guardsmen to help. Keith did not want the tanks to go on the reservation. In fact, he refused to let them in no uncertain terms. The man in charge got upset with Keith. Word got to the governor, then to the Regional Director in Albuquerque, then to the Agency Superintendent in Zuni, then back to Keith. By that time, the word had become, "Keith, what in the world are you doing? You have everyone upset. Even the governor called!"

"Well," Keith said, "How would you feel if you were snowed in your Hogan and then a big ugly tank with a gun on the front of it, the likes of which you had never seen before in your life, came crashing through the trees toward you?" Keith knew that many of the Navajo people had never even seen pictures of tanks. They had no electricity for TV. They did have a few battery-operated radios, but probably had never heard about an army tank. "Besides that," Keith continued, "do you want to rebuild all the cattle guards and fences they tear up? You will have people working all next summer repairing the damage they do." As it turned out, the tracks on the tanks contracted while they were sitting in the cold. One tank would not start. The other tank started but would not move because the tracks were too tight from contracting.

On the other hand, the helicopter was of great help. They needed someone who knew the reservation, so Keith went with them to drop hay to cattle and drop burlap bags with a five-day supply of food to the hogans. Before he had left the rancher who helped him, he had asked if he needed anything. Flour, coffee, and tobacco were his requests. Keith picked those things up along with some oranges. They flew over his house, waved for him to get back out of the way, and dropped him a burlap bag and the requested items. There was plenty of snow to cushion the fall of the bag!

They continued flying around to check on places where Keith thought would be the greatest need. They saw a man waving his arms frantically. Immediately grasping that this man was in trouble and needed help, they landed as near to him as they could. When they landed, the man came as fast as he could in the deep snow to the copter, climbed in, and using his finger to gesture, repeatedly pointed upward, indicating that he wanted to be taken up. As soon as they got up in the air, he began to gesture downward. He pointed to another hogan. Thinking that someone was hurt there and needed help, the pilot landed the helicopter. The man gave a big smile, said, "Akaha" (thank you), got out of the helicopter and walked toward the hogan. He had just wanted to get a ride! They hadn't gone but about a hundred feet.

It was obvious that the guardsmen knew little about cattle. They drove the four-wheel drive trucks out to the reservation and threw hay out in the snow, sometimes, a long way from the cattle. The cattle could not walk easily in the four-feet deep snow. Much of the hay was wasted.

The snow stayed on the ground several days…long enough for another teacher and me to take some free rides in the Ski-Doo that would finally work. Kenneth was old enough that he got a ride in it, too. Keith also saw to it that Kenneth got a ride in the helicopter.

When the snow finally melted, everyone had to fight mud. Long after the mud dried up, there was still a tank sitting beside the road in Ramah. It was the one that they couldn't get started. It stayed there for a few weeks. Every time we would go to town, we would remark, "Well, it looks like we still have that tank to help us out!" I thought it was going to rust before they finally took it away.

$\sim$

Finally, spring came, and with it, the feeling of outdoor freedom. We were glad to have the horses. Some evenings, Keith and I would take out riding up the canyon behind the school. Keith was always very daring. One evening, we found ourselves in a situation that the horses did not like. We were in a deep canyon, and it was so steep the horses didn't want to climb up the side. Keith pulled and pulled on them, one at a time, and told me to get behind and push. I didn't feel that it was safe and in addition, I was very weak and could hardly climb out myself. I'm not sure how we finally got them out, but by the time we did, night had settled in. Fortunately, there was a full moon and we could see fairly well. We were in a hurry to get back. We had left the boys with our neighbors. We ran the horses as they could take it and finally got home. It was about a week later that I found out that I was pregnant!

We had been married nine years. I had put the idea of giving birth out of my mind thinking that it probably would never happen. We had prayed about adopting the boys and felt that it was the Lord's will for us to do so whether or not biological children should come along. I know that God was watching over me. After all we went through with the horses, it would have been very easy for me to have had a miscarriage.

I was teaching second grade when I found out I was pregnant. It was tough teaching with morning sickness. My good friend in the classroom next door, Mrs. Bond, would sometimes have a

Sprite or 7Up on my desk with a poem of encouragement when I would arrive at school. Kenneth, our oldest son, was in kindergarten at the time. His teacher came to me one day and told me that he was worried because he heard his mommy crying each morning. I had to confess to her that I was expecting, and what he was hearing was his mommy throwing up in the bathroom. It wasn't so bad after the first three months. As I began to expand, I must have been a sight on the playground teaching the children how to play football by our made-up rules and exercising with them to a record when we stayed in on rainy days. Actually, I felt really good after the morning sickness subsided.

I was asked to be in charge of the school Christmas program. I tried to think of a way to have a good program without too much effort on the part of anyone. I decided on the theme "Joy to the World." This theme would be excellent for geography lessons. Each class was to select a country and come up with its own presentation of Christmas in that country. One of the upper classes made a huge round map of the world for the background with a large banner displaying the theme. Our sixth grade teacher had taught school in Germany, so it was a natural for her class to do Christmas in Germany. Our second grade class did Christmas in Hawaii. It was interesting to hear my Navajo students who had learned English as a second language singing the Hawaiian word for Merry Christmas! It was interesting, also, to hear the sixth graders speak in German knowing that many of those children also had learned English as a second language. We opened and closed the program by singing "Joy to the World." The program seemed to be a success.

◦

We did our shopping and doctoring in Gallup. Actually, the doctor was at Rehobath mission, another ten miles or so beyond Gallup. On one shopping trip, we saw a Navajo man that we knew walking beside the road. We picked him up to give him a ride back to Ramah. "Stop up here, Lamb, buy pop," he said. "Are you buying?" Keith asked him. I was shocked! To think that Keith would let this poor Navajo man spend his money when we could easily buy it. I kept quiet. McDaniel gave a soft little laugh and after a minute said, "Okay, I buy." We stopped at the trading post and McDaniel got out, went inside, and soon came back with pop for Keith, himself, and me. In addition, he had bought ice cream for the boys. He had a great big smile on his face. He felt so good to think that he was buying something for us! I learned a real lesson right then. One of the best things we can do to help people is to let them feel self worth. I sure had a laundry job when we got home, though. The boys had ice cream all over their clothes!

Everything seemed to be going well. We had purchased a Shasta camper and decided to take a trip to Phoenix the first of April for a little vacation. Kenneth's birthday is April 6, so we used the trip as a celebration for him as well. We bought him a bicycle, and he loved riding it around the park we had chosen to camp in. He was only five but was always big for his age and could easily handle it. He was also very intelligent and learned quickly. The four of us enjoyed the nice warm weather there. We parked the camper right beside an orange tree in bloom and could smell the odor of the blossoms through the window. We found a big field of flowers and Keith took my picture standing among the flowers. It is the only picture I have of being pregnant. It was a nice vacation.

All the way down to Phoenix, I had thought of nice juicy oranges. I was really craving oranges. I couldn't wait until we got there. Keith stopped at the first roadside fruit stand that we saw to buy me some oranges only to find that there were no oranges. We couldn't find oranges at any fruit stands. Finally, I settled for grapefruit. We bought a big twenty-five-pound bag of grapefruit, and I ate them all while we were in Phoenix. We bought another big bag to take home with us.

When we got back to Ramah, I was still enjoying grapefruit. I was afraid I was gaining too much weight. I would cut the grapefruit in half, sprinkle them with salt, and enjoy. I would wake up around 2 a.m. each night, go into the dining room, and sometimes, eat as many as ten grapefruit. On my next doctor's visit, I had lost several pounds of weight and was doing fine.

Keith had told a Navajo lady, Dorothy Antonio, that she might have to be my midwife. She would just grin when he would tell her. She had performed as such many times before, no doubt, but I wasn't comfortable with the idea.

School was finally out for the year, and I had more time to work on fixing up the third bedroom as a nursery. It was nice having time to do my own housework. Even though we had been blessed with an excellent young lady to take care of the boys and clean while I was teaching, every mother gets satisfaction from caring for her home.

Edith Garcia had worked in a motel before we met her. She had her routine down the way she wanted to do things. Every day, she would come, sit down, and read the paper or just sit until we left. When we left, she stripped all the beds, did laundry, mopped all the floors, dusted, and cleaned the kitchen. We had freshly laundered sheets to sleep on every night. Every day for lunch, Keith and the boys had tuna sandwiches. Keith got a little tired of tuna. Kenneth was glad when he started to kindergarten and got lunch at school. It was so nice to come home from work each day to a clean house. I could sit down and read to the boys and spend time with them. I had a clean kitchen to cook supper in. We still have the beautiful rug that Edith and her mom wove for us and gave us for Christmas.

Still, it was nice to be home and do my own cleaning. One Saturday, I mopped and waxed all the floors in the house and had every thing shining. Keith called and told me that the chapter president was coming for supper. I fixed barbequed chicken (baked in the oven) and had a nice big meal. After I had cleaned up from the meal, I felt something that I thought might be a labor pain. Keith had gone down to his office, so I called and told him that it might be time. Soon, I had another indication, and I phoned the doctor. He told me to come on to the hospital but there probably wasn't any reason to hurry. I made the mistake of telling Keith that he said there wasn't any hurry. He was with his friend, the academic department head, visiting outside somewhere on campus, and I couldn't find him. By that time, it was dark. Arvella, Ed's wife, went looking for them and finally found them.

We finally got started to the hospital, fifty miles away. Our neighbor was taking care of the boys. I began to feel what I thought were labor pains on the way and told Keith. We finally came to a stoplight at the edge of Gallup. There was a Navajo lady walking on the sidewalk up a hill. He began telling me about that lady. The light turned green, then red, then green again. I couldn't believe that he wasn't like most men who got frantic when they thought the baby was on the way. I was frightened. We still had ten or so miles to go.

Finally, after what seemed an eternity, we went on and arrived at the hospital. Trish was born at 4:45 the next morning, June 28, 1969. She was red in the face and chewing her fist and crying immediately. She was a perfect baby! She entered the world weighing 8 pounds and 14.5 ounces.

After I was settled in my room, Keith started back to Ramah. He hit a deer on the way home and damaged the car. Thankfully, no one was hurt. He came back later during the day to report that the boys were okay. I went home the next day. On the way home, Trish kept spitting up and I told Keith, "Looks like she is going to have trouble with car sickness." This turned out to be an accurate prophecy. She suffered with car sickness over and over as she grew up.

The ladies of the community had given me a shower. I had lots of nice things for her, including handmade crocheted and knitted blankets. I've always had a special appreciation for handwork. It was nice to have a little girl to dress up. Keith had said he wanted another boy, but this little girl wrapped him around her fingers. Three years later, when I found myself pregnant with Charles, he said he wanted a girl!

We liked being at Ramah and decided to buy a house instead of living in the government quarters. We bought the house of one of the sons of my teacher friend, Mrs. Bond. It was the first house we ever owned. We enjoyed it very much. We were in it only a short time when the agency superintendent mentioned the trouble they were having at the Albuquerque Indian School. Keith and the school at Ramah had just received a prestigious award. The secretary of the Department of the Interior had flown out from Washington, D.C. to present the award himself. The award included a bonus for each employee and Keith. He was feeling very confident after receiving the award and was quick to answer the agency superintendent. Keith said, "I could do a better job running that school than the present superintendent with one hand tied behind my back!" (Ah, the confidence of the young!) It began to look like a move to Albuquerque was in the future.

Sure enough, it wasn't long before Keith was requested to go and be the superintendent of Albuquerque Indian School. Since I was under contract to teach second grade, he moved the camper down to Albuquerque, and I stayed at Ramah with the children to finish out the school year.

Edith was no longer available to clean and care for the children. When she left us, we were fortunate to have a wonderful person, Ellen Stephens, the wife of one of the teachers, to care for the children while I was teaching. Her husband taught fourth grade, and they had lost a baby at birth. She treated our children as her own and truly loved them. I could again come home to a clean house and spend time with the children and fix dinner in a clean kitchen. Our oldest son, Kenneth, was always big for his age and had a talent for art. He loved to rearrange the furniture.

One day I came home and Ellen said, "Kenneth arranged the furniture so well, and it looked so nice that I decided to mop the kitchen floor!"

Even though we lived close to the school and could easily walk to work, it was difficult to do without the car. Keith needed it more in Albuquerque. I worried about the children getting sick and needing to take them to the doctor at Rehobath.

One afternoon, I came home from work to find that Trish was running a fever. I knew she needed to see the doctor. The only thing I could think of was to borrow a car from Mrs. Pace, one of the teachers. It was a Volvo…her pride and joy. I started to Rehobath mission where Trish had been born. About half way there, the window on the driver's side suddenly fell down inside the door. It was fairly cold with a few patches of snow left on the ground. I managed somehow to get a blanket up over the window. That helped a little to keep the cold air off of Trish.

We finally got to the mission and the waiting room was full. I asked for an aspirin to bring her fever down but was told they could not give her one until the doctor saw her. It seemed like an eternity before Trish's name was finally called. We were ushered into an examination room. Trish was sitting on my lap. The doctor looked into her throat and then looked in one ear. "This ear is infected," he said. Then he turned around to get a tool and looked back at Trish. He looked in the same ear again and said, "This ear doesn't look so bad." A disheveled mother was quickly losing confidence in this doctor! I called the mistake to his attention, and he quickly denied it. He went ahead and wrote a prescription for antibiotic. The mission also dispensed the medication, so I took Trish back to the waiting room to wait for the prescription to be filled. I asked the nurse for aspirin for her fever and again was refused. She was running a fever over 102 degrees.

Finally, our name was called for the prescription. I juggled Trish, the diaper bag and blankets and hurried to the window as quickly as possible, only to find that the medicine had been given to the lady in front of me, and she had already gone outside. I ran after her and caught her on the steps and retrieved the medicine.

I wondered what to do about the car window. I was already feeling badly that this had happened to a borrowed car. One of my rules was to never borrow a car from anyone, but circumstances had demanded that I do so. I decided to stop at a gas station to phone Mrs. Pace, to ask her what I should do. I was afraid she would say to get the window fixed while in Gallup. After all, it would be a real inconvenience for her to have to drive back forty miles to get it fixed. I rummaged in my purse for change for the pay phone. With Trish on my hip and holding her with one arm and trying to balance the receiver and at the same time put in the coins, I finally managed to dial the number. Just as Mrs. Pace said, "Hello," Trish threw up all over the desk of the owner of the gas station! Of course, the desk was covered with papers… no doubt very important papers. What did I do? I cried! On the other end of the line, Mrs. Pace was still saying "hello" with the sound of a question in her voice. I finally pulled myself together and told her about the window in her car. "Just bring it on," she said, "I'll have Dick Stephens take a look at it when you get here." I helped the angry station owner as much as I could and apologized over and over. At this point, I think he was as eager as I for me to be on my way and away from him! I made it home with no further incidents and immediately gave Trish some aspirin to bring her temp down.

᠀

Now that we knew for sure that we would be moving to Albuquerque, the task of finding a house there and selling the one we bought in Ramah loomed before us. Keith had contacted a realtor in Albuquerque and had been looking at houses. He wanted me to come down on a weekend to see some possibilities. I caught a ride with a teacher who was headed that way. On the way, Trish got car sick and threw up on the leather suede coat that my sister, Ernestine, had given me. Luckily, I was able to keep it off the teacher's car by sacrificing the coat. There was nothing I could do about the smell, however. I had brought her along because she was only eight months old, and I didn't think she was old enough to leave for the weekend. I had left the boys with the sitter, however.

When we got to Albuquerque, Keith was waiting for us in the Shasta camper. The appointment with the realtor was for Saturday, the next day. One of the houses was down Placitas Road in the Northwest Valley. We turned off Fourth Street and drove down a tree-lined shady street. At the very end of the street was this big, brick, sprawling ranch house with a circular drive and a gigantic blue spruce tree in the very front. The Spanish tile roof obviously needed to be replaced as the tiles were cracked and broken. The price of the house was exorbitant! It was $50,000! There was no way that I would be willing to pay that much for a house! I refused to look at it because I didn't think we could afford it. We drove on to other houses, but none seemed appropriate. Trish and I went back to Ramah on Sunday. Plans called for me to return on another weekend to look at more possibilities.

In the meantime, the son of my good friend who taught pre-first decided that they would like to buy our house in Ramah. It worked out perfectly for his family.

I got a call from Keith the next week telling me that he had put an offer in on the house that I refused to look at! I was flabbergasted! My first thought was that he had gone against my wishes and not considered what my opinion was. However, I kept quiet and listened as he described the inside for me. "It needs some work," he said. It was built by an attorney who was hired to work for President Nixon. The attorney moved to Washington, DC and had some young relatives live in the house after he moved. They had let their dog do some chewing on the door frame and generally had not taken care of the place. It had a huge kitchen. The den was lined with cedar with log beams across the top. Three bedrooms were at one end of the house separated from the kitchen by the living room and dining room. The attorney who had built the house did a great deal of entertaining. A large patio extended across the back of the house with two brick barbeque pits. A brick planter surrounded the patio. Two workshops separated the living area from the double-car garage. "There is a fortune in landscaping," he said. There were many roses planted in brick planters under the kitchen window. The lot was 7/8 acre with plenty of room for a garden. There was a little greenhouse in the backyard. A cherry tree and apple tree made the place even more appealing. Grapevines covered the fence that separated the lot from the large irrigation ditch. The tall poplars provided a great deal of privacy for the backyard. It was a special place! I reluctantly said that it sounded good while feeling a little fear that we really couldn't afford it.

Keith went ahead and consummated the deal, and we were the proud owners of 288 Placitas Road, NW. All we had to do was for me to finish the year teaching and start packing.

As soon as the school year was over, we moved to Albuquerque

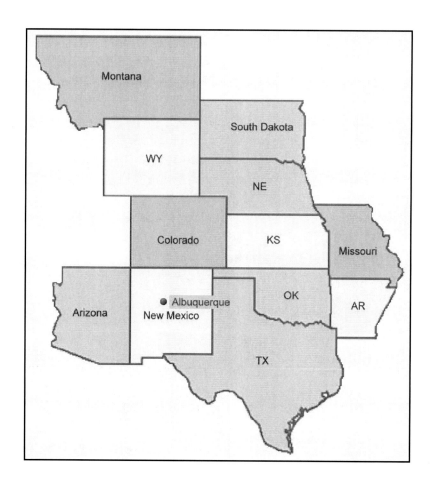

"With One Hand Behind my Back!"

Albuquerque, New Mexico

*I*t was exciting to move into such a big, pretty, unique house. We had often joked that you could go into any government quarters and be blindfolded and still find your way around because the floor plans were all so much alike. The rambling ranch floor plan of this house was interesting. The kitchen, dining room, and den were at one end of the house, and the bedrooms and two bathrooms were at the other end. A huge living room was in the middle of the house. Even though we had bought our first house in Ramah, this one was much different and very much a new experience for us. We began to do some fixing up since the couple who had been staying there did not take good care of it. One of the first things we did was put in new carpets. When we put new carpets in the living room, dining room, and hallway, it took ninety square yards of carpet. There were two fireplaces, one in the den and one in the living room. The back of the living room was all glass windows from the floor to the ceiling. The boys had their own bedroom, and Trish had a room. The master bedroom had a walk-in closet with a mirror, cedar cabinets, and dressing area. I never dreamed I would have a house so nice. It did, however, need a new roof. It took us some time to get enough Spanish tiles to reroof the house, and it was quite expensive to do so. In spite of this, we knew that the Lord had blessed us with a special home.

There was a small greenhouse in the backyard, as well as a cherry tree and grapevines. We had a large garden area and a pen where we could raise an animal or two. The house was located in the valley at the edge of town so zoning code permitted animals. We lived there for nine years and during that time, raised two steers to butcher, chickens, and goats. We had a garden each year, and I did much canning and food preservation. It was like living in the city and country at the same time. The children enjoyed the big yard and the nice neighbors. Since we were on a cul-de-sac, it was pretty safe and very private.

When we finally felt settled in, Keith received word that the Ramah Navajo people had requested that he come back to Ramah. My heart sank. Although we liked Ramah, we felt it was time to move on. The powers that be decided to keep Keith in Albuquerque.

Keith had both of his hands full with his job. High school Indian students were sent to Albuquerque Indian School from reservations throughout the country. He soon learned that, quite often, they were the kids causing trouble at home, and they were sending them away to get rid of them. He had a fairly good staff and budgeted over a million dollars which was quite a bit for that time. Because there was a psychologist on the staff, it seemed that people on the reservations thought troubled youth could be better dealt with in Albuquerque. The school had several buildings and quite a large staff. The ratio of students to worker was six to one.

On one occasion, the school received two new students before their files with information about them arrived. Keith received a call in his office from one of the dormitories and was told that one of those students had a gun. Keith advised the dormitory aide to send the students to his office. He watched out his office window as two young men came walking slowly across the campus to his office. He noticed they were talking to each other rather secretively and were trying to conceal something. When they walked in the office, one of the boys immediately pointed a gun at Keith. With the gun pointed at him, he walked around behind his desk and called the police. The police came immediately, within about five minutes, Keith said. Upon arrival, one policeman dropped to his knees, pointed a gun at the student and said, "Drop it!" The boy hesitated and the policeman cocked his gun. The student was looking all around the room and especially at the window. Finally, he dropped the gun. The policeman took it, and emptied the bullets out of it.

I was at home doing the weekly ironing when the phone rang. "Pat," Keith said, "What have you heard?" I didn't know what he was talking about. Since I didn't have the TV on, I didn't know that it was on the news. Keith said he wanted to call me and let me know that he was okay. Later, he told me that he thought there might have been angels in his office protecting him and wondered if that was why the student kept looking frantically all around the room. Also, he thought that the boy was considering jumping through the window since the policeman had the doorway blocked. When Keith called the police, he didn't know that the gun was really loaded. He was surprised to see the policeman empty the bullets on his desk.

When Keith finally received the files on the boys, he found that one of them had burned a building down on the reservation where he had lived. He felt it was that boy who had talked the other into using the gun and that the boy who had the gun was allowing himself to be talked into something he shouldn't have.

There were many powwows at the Indian School. Each time, we were guests of honor and presented with gifts. On one occasion, I was home and Keith attended alone. I had the TV on and saw Miss Indian America present a beautiful Pendleton blanket to Keith, put it around him, and give him a kiss. He was sure smiling!

When we had been in Albuquerque about three years, I found out I was pregnant. I was feeling as though I was a bad mother and was quite apprehensive about the responsibility of another child. David was not enthused about school. He was in second grade and his teacher was calling me every night to see if he got home with his homework. Every night, I would sit and work with him on his math. Although I had taught all the kids to count fairly well and to read some before they started to school, Dave was not doing well. We would sit at the kitchen table each night to work on his math homework. I would use miniature marshmallows, popcorn, spaghetti, or whatever I could think of to try to make it interesting for him. We would put down ten, take away three and see how many were left. The phone would invariably ring while I was trying to get him to concentrate. I was WMU (Woman's Missionary Union) director at the church, and it seemed that I got many calls concerning church work. "Keep working, Dave, and I'll be back in a little bit," I would tell him. When I would come back, there would not be one more problem done, and he would have eaten the objects! I was exasperated!

Kenneth and Trish were doing well in school, but trying to keep up with housekeeping and church work, as well as taking care of the three, already had made me wonder if I could handle another.

Once again, the Lord demonstrated His understanding. When Charles was born, he was the best baby ever! He was so easy to care for. As a toddler, I would say, "Charles, it's time for your nap." I would hand him a bottle and he would go to his crib, climb in, and go to sleep. The Lord always knows what we can handle. The day I came home from the hospital, two very dear friends, June Brewer and Vivian Andrews, came and waited on me. They cleaned the house and treated me like a queen. I will never forget those two friends.

*

We bought a piano when Kenneth was in second grade, and started lessons for him. He took to it like a duck to water. He caught on so fast that I asked his teacher to put him through two series of books to develop the muscles in his hands. He was learning the pieces so fast that he would have them accomplished before his hands got the exercise they should. He continued to do well and played for the graduation at the Indian School when he was ten years old. He played "Pomp and Circumstance" for the graduates to march in and later played "Berceuse" and "The Entertainer," by Scott Joplin.

Later, we bought a used organ, and I started playing it. The pastor at our little church talked me into playing the organ at the church there. Since that time, I have played in other churches as well. I do not consider myself a very good organist, but I certainly have enjoyed playing at home. When I play, I feel like I am worshiping.

Trish was asked to be a cheerleader at the Indian School when she was five. She was a pretty little thing with long blonde hair down to her waist. She was the mascot with the Indian girls cheering. To this day, she hasn't forgiven me for not allowing her to wear shorts. She wore long pants. Her cheering with the girls was a visual demonstration of integration at its best with the coal black hair of the Indian girls and the bright shiny blonde little girl cheering with them!

At one of the football games, during halftime, the band suddenly started playing "Happy Birthday." Keith had asked them to play it for me. I felt that was really special to have everyone at the game wishing me a happy birthday. The announcer even announced it over the loud speaker!

As superintendent, Keith was asked to participate in many things. He was even asked to help judge a beauty contest in the city. We attended many banquets. It seemed strange to always sit at the head table.

It was not unusual for the school to have visitors from Washington, DC. On one occasion, Elizabeth Dole and some of her staff visited. They were asking if the school needed more money. Keith surprised them by saying no. He explained that the school had a ratio of six students to each staff member, had closed-circuit television, had a machine that would graph eye movements for a student when reading, and that they were really doing quite well. On another occasion, Bobby Kennedy came to the school and requested that leaders of various tribes meet there with him for a news conference. He requested TV cameras be there. His main topic was water rights of the tribes. He began talking and could get none of the leaders to agree with anything. Keith said that Mr. Kennedy finally got red in the face and told the TV people to leave. He left rather abruptly and went on his way. He didn't realize, I suppose, that through the ages, there has been a great deal of animosity between tribes and that it is very difficult to get them to work together.

Keith was given an invitation to Jimmy Carter's inauguration. We attended. A friend kept the kids for us. Keith went on ahead, and I flew to join him. I remember how cold it was that year. As the plane flew over Kansas City, I looked down and saw the boats enclosed in ice on the Missouri River. At the inauguration, people were putting newspapers down on the ice and snow as we stood and listened to the inaugural address and watched the ceremony. The newspaper gave a bit of insulation for our feet. We watched the parade and walked and walked and walked. I had some pretty sore feet when it was over, and they were numb with cold. We attended First Baptist Church on the Sunday following the inauguration and watched as the president, Rosalyn, and Amy joined the church. When I had to go to the restroom, I passed some of the secret service men. I overheard one say, "I guess we'll have to go to church all the time with this president!" I couldn't resist. I had to say something. "Good," I said. "That will be good for you!"

We were impressed by the mood in DC. Each of the Smithsonian buildings had bluegrass concerts of gospel music. When we got on the bus, people were polite and would offer you their seat. All through the city, it seemed like there were a lot of Christian people attending the inauguration. We saw lots of homeless people on the sidewalks sleeping over the grates where warm steam was coming out. I felt sad about that. When we got home, we had much to tell.

✺

When Kenneth went into seventh grade, we felt that we needed to be in a larger church where there would be a good youth program. We had been attending Boulevard Baptist Church located not too far from us. It was a neighborhood church. We joined First Baptist Church located in downtown Albuquerque. The pastor, Dr. Morris Chapman, asked me to work on the staff part-time as outreach director. I loved it. He asked me to fly to Memphis, Tennessee to observe an outreach program at Belleview Baptist Church that Adrian Rogers was doing there and bring ideas back to our church. We called the program the King's Command. About sixty people, as I recall, signed up for the program the first time around. On Sunday evenings, the pastor would give a lesson on witnessing. I prepared notes and notebooks for each person and did the paperwork. During the week, on each Tuesday night, the group was divided according to the quadrants of the city and met in homes before going out to visit. I took turns going to the different quadrants and would sometimes give the devotional before we went out to visit. The program was very successful.

I was also asked to be WMU director. I didn't feel that I could handle the job with everything else I was doing and finally agreed to be assistant WMU director, in charge of the Acteens, GAs (Girls in Action), and Mission Friends. We did a father-daughter banquet, and later, awards recognition for the organizations. It was such a thrill to watch the fathers bring their little girls all dressed up to the banquet. The fathers would pull out the chairs for the girls and open doors for them. We wouldn't let the staff take part in the program because we felt that the pastor, song leader, and others should be free to enjoy their daughters.

A nursery loaned us lots of flats of flowers, so the dining room was decorated gloriously. We made up our own lyrics to familiar songs, and the girls sang to their dads. One song had lyrics that said, "I am sixteen, going on seventeen. Dad, I'll depend on you." The awards recognition was just as nice. One highlight of the program was an Indian lady singing "The Lord's Prayer" while another Indian girl signed it. It was very touching.

During the '70s, when we were in Albuquerque, the country was experiencing riots. On one occasion, students from the University of New Mexico marched down Main Street throwing bricks through the windows of storefronts, etc. We were very surprised to be watching this on TV and seeing the face of the son of one of the instructional aides we had at Lukachukai at the front of the group. He was the same little boy who had accidentally set fire to the curtains in his family's apartment at the end of the dorm.

There was a great deal of crime in Albuquerque. We had an unpleasant experience one afternoon when I had decided to take the children to a friend's house to go swimming. When we returned home and came in through the kitchen door, I immediately noticed my squash blossom necklace lying on the kitchen table. My first thought was that Keith had come home and had been showing it to someone. When I walked on into the dining room, I noticed a screen off the window standing on the floor and leaning up against the wall. Someone had pried open the window and come into the house! I went on into the bedroom and saw our small gray file barely showing from under the bed as though someone had slung it on the floor. Someone had been in the dressing room and been rifling through the cabinets.

I phoned Keith at the Indian School and then phoned the police. The police came and took fingerprints and looked around. The crook had left clear black fingerprints on the white wall where he had climbed in the window of the dining room. Keith checked and found his watch with the turquoise and silver band, his CO_2 gun, another gun or two, and some bolo ties missing.

The policeman told us that it looked like a certain person's work. He said that person rode up and down Fourth Street on a bicycle. However, the children and I remembered that the day before a man had come to the door looking for the lawyer who lived next door. I thought it strange at the time that he wasn't looking for him at his office instead of his home in the middle of the afternoon. I had a hunch that something wasn't right, and I had the children write down the license number of the car. In spite of this, the police never found who did it. We were told that they had such a backlog of crimes to investigate that they seldom could follow one through. We did, however, get lots of calls from people wanting to sell us security systems and guns. One individual called Keith and said he had a gun like the one that was stolen and wondered if he wanted to buy it.

The children were afraid to go in the house alone for months after that. When we would go someplace and come home, I had to go in first to make sure it was safe before they would go in. I was glad we didn't walk in on the person. One of the guns he stole was loaded. Keith had left it loaded for our protection!

∽

One young man at the Indian school was the pride and joy of the staff. He had such good manners! Keith was always trying to find creative ways to help the students. This young man knew karate, so Keith organized a class of the female employees to take lessons from him to learn to protect themselves.

"In this class, I am not your friend, I am your teacher!" he told the ladies. They loved him and enjoyed the class. He was a senior and was getting ready to graduate. His Navajo parents sent him some money to buy clothes for graduation. He took the money and bought alcohol. He got drunk and walked out in front of a big truck on the highway and was killed. That was one of the few times since I have known Keith that I saw him cry. He sat on the couch silently crying with tears running down his cheeks. He got in the government car and drove all the way to the northern part of the Navajo reservation to tell the parents. It was really hard for him!

Keith used funds to buy painting supplies for the students to use. Many of the students were very artistic. They would paint pictures and do math problems by figuring out the cost of paint, labor, etc. Arrangements were made for a display of paintings from the school at the shopping mall. We purchased some of them and still have them in our home.

A reading company asked Keith to go to Guam to talk about the program they were using at the school. I told him to be sure and take some pictures because I knew that I would never be able to go there. He phoned me early one morning from Hawaii on his way back home to tell me he had left Guam early because a typhoon was coming in. "Don't worry," he said. "I'm okay. I got out in time, and I'm in no danger from the volcano erupting here!" I was certainly glad when he got home.

Some Indian people had been buried in makeshift graves near the school. Keith made sure that proper stones were placed on the graves.

The students made some jewelry as well as doing the painting. A thief came one morning and stole some of the jewelry. Keith took after him and chased him on foot a couple of blocks. He saw a police car, flagged it down, turned in the thief and got the jewelry back.

The elementary school where David and Trish attended was a good school. The middle school and high school left much to be desired. We were concerned about Kenneth because he was now middle school age. We decided to enroll him in Albuquerque Academy. To pay the tuition, I decided to substitute teach. I soon learned that I was being sent to classes where the teacher could not handle the children. That was tough! In the meantime, Kenneth was having trouble getting along with the affluent white kids at the academy. They were asking him to do a rain dance, etc. Kenneth's personality was not the kind to take those things lightly. He was having a tough time, and I was having a tough time.

We took Kenneth out of the academy and put him back in public school. He joined the Albuquerque Youth Symphony and played bass as well as accompanying the symphony on the piano for some pieces. We were so proud of him! He also played the piano to accompany the presentation of "Charlie Brown" at the Valley High School. Trish and Charles were doing very well. We decided to hold David back a year in school. He was very bright, but he didn't seem to have the academic interest needed to complete his assignments. We discovered that David needed to wear eyeglasses when he was in second grade. It seemed that, all through school, it was *push* and *pull*. We thought that holding him back a year would make it easier, and he would enjoy school more. I think it helped, but it did not solve the problem.

৵৹

Those old enough will remember the turmoil in our country during the '70s. Some of the Indian people were showing some resentment toward the white man. There was a big push to get the white man out of the Bureau of Indian Affairs. Although most of the Indian people did not feel this way, as is often the case, the noisy ones got the attention. Much had been accomplished at the Indian School, but because Keith was white, a demand was made to turn over this school along with many others to the Indian people. Keith was reassigned to work in Washington, DC, temporarily.

He had already been given the responsibility of educational director for the Southern Pueblo Agency along with being super-intendent of the Indian School. Now, he was to go to DC on a three-month appointment to work on budgeting for the Bureau of Indian Affairs. Since it was to be for only three months, we didn't feel it feasible to move there. However, three months turned into one and a half years as they kept renewing his temporary appointments. He came home when he could, usually every two or three weeks for the weekend. It was not easy taking care of the children by myself. By this time, Kenneth was in high school and David was getting ready to enter junior high. They needed a daddy home with them. Trish and Charles were doing fine.

Finally, the Indian School was contracted out under Indian supervision. Keith transferred from the Bureau of Indian Affairs to the Office of Surface Mining. We moved to the Kansas City area.

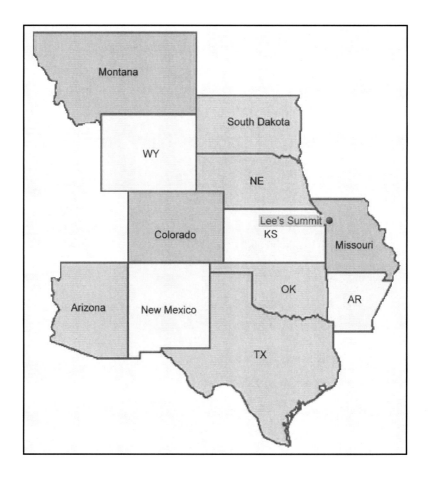

Back to the Green Country Again!

Lee's Summit, Missouri

We were in Kansas City for a relatively short time. We found a home in Lee's Summit, Missouri, in a subdivision called Lakewood. It was midway between Lee's Summit, Raytown, Independence, and Blue Springs. It was a nice subdivision. It was a secured location, and the security guard was on duty to drive around and make sure everything was going well. Since he went to the same church that we did, the kids all knew they had better not do anything wrong or we would find out about it. There was a lake there. Our youngest son, Charles, was now in second grade. He would come home from school and walk down to the lake and catch fish before supper.

When we were looking for our home, the real estate agent had driven us through the subdivision and talked about the snooty people there. We passed one house for sale and he said, "That house has been on the market a long time. I know why it hasn't sold. There is a black family that lives next door." I said, "That wouldn't bother us at all." He didn't seem to hear me and never set up the time to show us the house. We were having a hard time with him, so Keith contacted another agent and asked to see the house. We bought it. We found it all to be in God's plan.

We attended Oakwood Baptist Church while there, and I served as church secretary. It was a community church located at the edge of the subdivision. Right away, it was obvious that there were many young people in the community who needed activities and were not involved in church. We needed a boys' softball team! All of the men in the church were busy with their jobs. Most had to commute to Kansas City and that left little time for extra activities.

Kenneth continued to study piano under Gladys Alkire and went through his virtuoso books. We enjoyed his recitals.

Our son, David, was in the eighth grade, and he was making friends with the boy next door who was also in eighth grade. They had several friends in the subdivision. After praying about it, I told the boys that I would be their coach for a church softball team if they would do all the work of phoning the players for practice, etc. David and Dalton, the black boy next door, were cocaptains and would always do the calling and notify the other guys. The boys would ride their bikes to our house, park them all in our yard, jump in the back of our red El Camino, and I would drive them to church in the afternoons after school to practice. We must have been a sight! The El Camino had a silly horn on it, and I would honk it all the way to the church. We had lots of fun!

The first year, all of my boys were in the eighth grade but one. Our pitcher was a seventh grader. We played in the church league with, as I recall, five other teams. We ignored the fact that racial prejudice existed. All of the boys were white except the cocaptains. Our son, David, was Northern Cheyenne. Dalton, the other cocaptain who lived next door, was black. No one ever showed any signs of even noticing the difference.

Keith was free on Saturdays and agreed to go to the games with us and be an umpire.

The first game was a memorable one. When we got there, the coach of the other team immediately went to Keith to talk to him about his team. Keith said, "There's your coach, over there." When he pointed to me, a funny look came on the face of the coach of the other team. His tongue went into his cheek, and

I couldn't really tell if he was trying to keep from laughing out loud or if he was thinking, "This should be an easy win!" As is the case with many church teams, it looked like his team had taken anyone who had a warm body and was male. One of his players had a US Marine Corps T-shirt on. You could tell he had been shaving for some time.

When the game started, all of my guys were trying to kill the ball and be a big hero. They began to strike out. I didn't know a great deal about softball and its rules, but I did know that their pitcher was not that good. He was pitching wild balls. I called my boys aside and said, "Look, guys, a walk is as good as a run. Let him walk you. If you watch him, you can see that he is not throwing many strikes." It took a while to get them settled down, but soon they began to catch on and they got some walks. We began to score.

When the big guy with the Marine T-shirt got up to bat, he motioned my center-fielder to one side. Then he motioned for him to back up. I suspected he was trying to show off a bit. My center fielder did just what he was told to do. The pitch was thrown, the ball was hit to just that spot, and my center fielder caught it and put him out! It was hilarious!

We won that game by a narrow margin, and there was no holding my guys back after that. They knew they could do it! We went the rest of the season playing similar teams who were older and much more experienced. While their coaches would be biting their lips to keep from swearing (since, after all, it was a church league) I would be yelling, "All right, guys, no more cookies for you!" Sometimes, I would yell and tell them something to do, and they would smile and say, "Mrs. Lamb, you can't do that. That's against the rules." One of my players came up with so many signals that we couldn't remember them all. Finally, I got him to eliminate some of them. On a few occasions, they would yell at me from their positions on the field, "If we win this, can we stop for pizza on the way home?"

After practice in the afternoons, I would sometimes take them into the church building, so they could get a drink, and we would sit in the auditorium and rest as I played "Onward Christian Soldiers" or "Battle Hymn of the Republic" on the organ. They seemed to enjoy it. Some of the boys started coming to church. On one occasion, Dalton, the boy from next door was at our house waiting for David for some activity they had in mind. At the kitchen table, we went over the plan of salvation. He told me that he had been saved in a black church in downtown Kansas City when he was younger but had never been baptized. He was baptized at our church and attended regularly. When he graduated from high school, the church gave him a scholarship to Southwest Baptist College (now university) in Bolivar.

We took third place in the league that summer. The next summer, we tied for first place. By this time, there were six softball teams going at our church. Some of us decided it would be nice to have a sports banquet at the end of the season. It was planned and turned out to be a big success. James Jeffries, who was affiliated with the Fellowship of Christian Athletes, spoke at our banquet. He told how his two sons played college football and one had played for the San Diego Chargers in the NFL (National Football League). In his story, he told how he required his sons to always write their goals and that the goal of one son was to be a quarterback in the NFL. He said that his son would practice throwing the football at a pole on the school ground every night after school. Then at the end of the story, he told why it was so hard for him to let his son do that. He was afraid he would be disappointed since he stuttered and would have a hard time with the cadence. The son went on to play for Baylor, and the newspapers made fun of him because he had to sing his cadence, but he reached his goal and did play in the NFL.

At the banquet, one of my players went up front and made a speech and asked me to come up front. My team surrounded me and presented me with a cut glass condiment dish. They had gone shopping and picked it out themselves. Needless to say, I will always treasure that dish.

After that banquet, we would see Dalton behind his house on the vacant lot throwing the football almost every night. When he went to Southwest Baptist College, he played football, and they had a great team. After we had moved to Denver, and back to Missouri, we were watching TV one night and saw him on TV. He was the quarterback for the team. The last I heard, he had graduated from school there and was managing a sporting goods store in Lee's Summit.

Jimmy Carter was president at this time, and there was a moving around of government workers. Keith was going to be transferred to another location. He received word that he was going to be transferred to Laramie, Wyoming. I resigned as church secretary and applied for a teaching job there, so I could go on and get the kids in school at the beginning of the year. I was not accepted for the job, and it was a good thing. Everything got stalled, and we didn't go anywhere for a while. Now I had no work. We were at the Independence Mall one day, and Trish saw a sign that said "Help Wanted" at the Singer Sewing Center in the Hancock Fabric Store. "Mom, you should apply," she said, "you like to sew." I applied and got the job. I worked there until we could find out for sure where Keith was being transferred. I sold only a few sewing machines but my name came out in the newsletter that I was a top salesperson in a certain area. I don't know how that happened. They must not have been selling many machines.

Finally, Keith's "for sure" papers came through, and we were to move to Denver. The kids had really liked the area, as did Keith. Trish had played softball on a church team, and Charles had been on a swim team. All of the kids had been on soccer teams. They all hated to leave. We had bought a boat, and they had all learned to water ski. Even I had learned to ski and enjoyed it. I didn't mind leaving that four-level house, however. It seemed that I was always separated from the rest of the family. Also, I had spent eight days in the hospital with lower abdomen pain in Lee's Summit. I was ready to forget about that experience. Kenneth joined the army prior to our leaving. Keith, David, Trish, Charles, and I went to Denver.

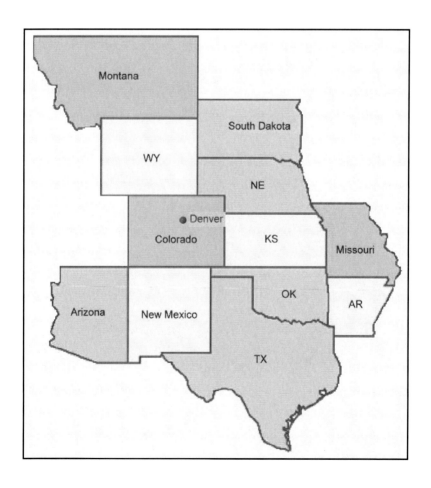

Back out West

Denver, Colorado

$\mathcal{I}$nterest rates were very high, and we were unable to sell our house in Lee's Summit for a long time. We found another house in Aurora, Colorado, in Mission Viejo, and put an earnest money deposit down on it. We got permission to move in. Keith's boss had been required to transfer, too. He was having a hard time selling his house, also. We had put most of our money into the house in Lee's Summit and were having a hard time financially. His boss lived with us and paid us rent. He ate with us at our family meals. It was Charles' job to clear the table. We had a hard time teaching Charles to wait until everyone was through eating. Dave and Trish would giggle as he would impatiently stand beside Keith's boss waiting for him to finish.

I took a job at So-Fro Fabrics at the nearest shopping mall. I had always enjoyed sewing and thought this might be a way I could help out with our finances. It was hard work! As much as I loved fabric, I really didn't enjoy lifting those large bolts and being on my feet all day. I can still remember how my feet would ache at night. Many times, I couldn't get to sleep because my feet were hurting so badly. In addition, my boss was the kind of boss who liked to feel important and show authority. I got along with her satisfactorily, but it wasn't easy. To top it all off, I was embarrassed when the teenagers would go to the cash register with no fear and quickly press in the numbers when sales were made. My teaching background had given me the habit of always trying to understand everything, and I found myself being overly cautious. Instinctively, I would figure the amounts in my head double-checking the register! That slowed me down, and I felt like I wasn't doing well enough. My conscientious nature probably caused me to imagine that I was inferior, but it was a good lesson to me that teenagers can do well when the desire is there.

We attended Riverside Baptist Church in downtown Denver. I taught the ladies' class. One lady in the church had been cleaning houses and was tired of it. To get more money, I took some of the houses to clean that she no longer wanted. I cleaned houses, took care of our own house, cooked for Keith's boss, and tried to be the best mother I could.

The real estate agent was trying to get us to get a bridge loan but we knew better than that. We got out of that contract and moved into a rental…a very small rental. It was so bad that later, a friend confessed that she and another lady had walked by the backyard and the lady had said, "I would cry if I had to live in that house!" The yard was overgrown with a good crop of dandelions. There were three bedrooms and two baths upstairs, a living room, dining area, kitchen and family room downstairs. There was a double car garage where most of our things remained unpacked for the duration of the time we lived there. I remember how sad I was that I couldn't get all the Christmas decorations out that Christmas. We were pretty crowded in that house.

We got busy trying to fix up the place. I paid the kids a penny for every dandelion they dug up in the yard. We put a hardwood floor in the kitchen and eating area. Finally, we saved enough money to buy the place. The lady who sold us the house we had rented talked to me about getting my real estate license. I decided to do it since it was a fairly short course. I quit the cleaning jobs and the fabric store job and got a job substitute teaching at Excelsior Youth Center for girls while I got my real estate license. These were girls who had been in trouble. One of the girls had been accused of aiding her brother in killing their parents. Some were runaways from home. Working there was an interesting experience. The girls would be acting fine and suddenly go off. They might start running down the hall and knocking down hanging plants, etc. Then, they would have to go to lock-up. I did little more than be present since they wanted two adults at all times with the girls. I got bored because I felt I was accomplishing so little.

I got my real estate license and went to work for Century 21 when the interest rates were 16 percent. I decided that people needed a place to live no matter what the rates were. To me, I was simply matching people with their needs. The first year, I was a million dollar producer. That doesn't sound like much now. The average price of a home in Denver then was around $76,000. Now, of course, it is much higher. Nevertheless, I did fairly well. I received several awards for both listings and sales. The house in Lee's Summit, Missouri, finally sold and with my earnings, we were able to buy a more adequate house for our family. We used the one we were in as an investment and later sold it to the people who were renting it.

When President Reagan was elected, things began to change. Interest rates began to come down, and I continued to do well with sales. I bought into the company and got my broker's license. My partner and I secured a larger building and we had, as I recall, about twelve agents. Denver began to take a downturn, however, when most of the country seemed to be thriving. Things went well in spite of the large number of foreclosures that were taking place there. I remember opening the newspaper and seeing a section of the paper listing foreclosures.

Keith's office was downtown, and he had to commute each day. The schools were fairly good, but David had a hard time figuring everything out in the big high school. He was very intelligent, but had little interest in some of the things required. Finally, we allowed him to drop out and get his GED. He passed the test easily and met with a recruiter to join the army. He had always had a special interest in war. He spent his extra money buying books about WWII and war equipment.

Keith seemed to have to travel a great deal again as he was being used to go on Indian reservations to reclaim mining land. Charles was in a year-round school, and, occasionally, was able to go with his dad. When he was sent to the Navajo reservation on one trip, I went with him. Several years had passed since our days at Lukachukai. Now, there was a motel at Pinion and we stayed there. There was actually good reception of TV there. On Sunday morning, we listened and watched a Navajo minister preach on TV using the Navajo language. Keith suddenly started laughing. (Keith understood more of the language than I). "He said that if you don't know Christ, you are no better than that dung behind a sheep on the ground," Keith explained.

Keith was so good about cooking when he was home on the weekends. The kids got lots of bean burritos. He would make up a batch on the weekend, with their help, and freeze them. The kids had them as snacks when they came home from school in the afternoons. My busy schedule in real estate made it difficult for me to prepare good meals.

Tricia was doing very well at Smoky Hill High School. She was in the color guard. They won several awards, and she looked so pretty in her Scottish uniform. She was on the honor roll each semester.

We lived in Denver for about nine years. Keith decided to retire. By this time, David was in the army and Trish was in college. Keith and Charles wanted to move to Missouri. I was doing well in real estate and was hesitant to move. They convinced me, and we did so. I prayed about it, and in my mind, I envisioned a bed and breakfast where we could witness to guests and serve homemade jams, jellies, etc.

Keith and I flew to Missouri and started looking for houses. Keith had contacted the real estate agent who happened to be the one playing the part of the old shepherd in the Shepherd of the Hills pageant in Branson. I had referred us to the Century 21 office in Branson from our Century 21 office in Denver. He was showing us terrible places. At lunch time, I said, "Why don't you let me see your MLS (Multiple Listing Service) book, and maybe I can save lots of time." He didn't want to do that, but I kept insisting. I found a place listed for much more than we wanted to pay, but it had the comment, "May sell a portion." I showed it to him. He had to be at practice for his acting part that evening, and he was hesitant to take us all the way to Lampe to see the place. We talked him into it and decided to make an offer. I was embarrassed at the offer Keith made for the whole place (113 acres). We both thought the offer would be refused, but it was accepted. I had sold out my interest in the real estate office a few months before and was only being a salesperson. I had some houses under contract, so it would be necessary to conduct business from Missouri by phone to finish the deals.

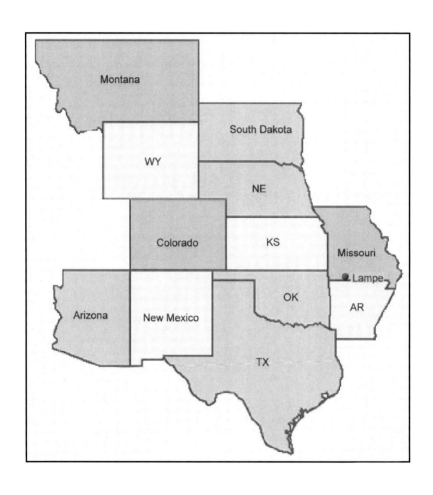

Home Territory

Lampe, Missouri

*O*nce again, we had a place that needed much work. Charles and I "camped out" in the house and Keith stayed in Denver to close on our house there, as he had a few more weeks to go on his job before the retirement date. It was in the heat of the summer, and there were lots of weeds in the yard. The couple who had lived there were in their eighties and the place was a mess. I burned the curtains in the family room. Charles and I had sleeping bags and slept on the floor in the back part of the house that seemed a little cleaner. I had forgotten how terrible chiggers could be in Missouri, and I got covered with them. I had a bottle of rubbing alcohol, and one night, I began to dab alcohol on all my chigger bites. Soon I was shivering and shaking. For a moment, I couldn't figure out why I was so cold. Then it dawned on me. I had put so much alcohol on my bites that I had given myself an alcohol bath!

The house was an interesting place. Part of it was built in 1891–92 of hand-hewn limestone. We were told that one of the men who helped build the Crescent Hotel in Eureka Springs, Arkansas, had built it. He had been paid two cows, two horses, and a pig for his work. It had sat empty for a number of years before the previous owners bought it and began fixing it up. Animals had actually been downstairs. There was an article in the Kansas City Star about the restoration done by the previous owners. There were initials carved in the limestone and a date was carved on one stone showing the time it was built. One person told us that Bonnie and Clyde had stayed there while passing through the area. The previous owners had built on to the stone part of the house and had basically lived in the part they built. There was an old wood stove in the family room in the older part of the house. A green carpet of the kind once popular in kitchens was in the family room. Hay had actually been stored in it at one time. It was dirty!

Charles and I went to Cassville and ordered oak flooring. I purchased carpet and had it laid for the part of the house that had been added. We did what we could to the place until Keith and the furniture arrived. We piled all the furniture in one end of the house. When Keith got there, the oak flooring arrived, and we began to lay it. My nephew and his wife came with a machine to remove the carpet and scraped up the old carpet in the family room. There was no air conditioning in the family room. We had rags wrapped around our wrists and foreheads to keep the sweat from dripping on the boards. Our oldest son, Kenneth came home and was a big help. I would pick out the boards, Keith would measure them, Kenneth would cut them, and Keith would nail them in place. Charles would "spell" us.

We put hardwood floors in the family room and in one bedroom. When we got the boards all laid, we sanded and varnished them. There was wood paneling and the dust from the sanding got in the crevices of that. I used Lemon Pledge and a brush and went over all the walls.

Trish had been in college in Denver and met her future husband. She was planning a wedding at the glass cathedral in Eureka Springs. She had wanted to be married in a small country church, so I took the phonebook and began calling local churches. Every church I called didn't want their church to be used by someone who wasn't a member, so we opted for the glass cathedral in Eureka Springs. She was to be married in September and it was already summer. We expected we would need to have the place ready for guests by the time of the wedding.

We made it. In fact, we had our first guests for the bed and breakfast even before that. Our first guests were four cousins whose grandfather had lived there. They were related to the people who had homesteaded the property in 1891. We had named our bed and breakfast, Grandpa's Farm. How appropriate! It seemed an indication that we were following God's plan.

One of our first guests was a gentleman who had come to check out a child from Kanakuk Kamp, located three miles away. When we talked to him, we learned for the first time about the camp. Then, we knew why God had led us to this place. We were the nearest place for parents to stay when they came to check out their kids from the Christian sports camp. In the fifteen years that we had the B and B, we met many wonderful Christian people from many places. We had many opportunities to witness to others not associated with the camp as well. We have many stories related to guests who said they were "led" to our B and B.

We started the Bed and Breakfast with only one room to rent. It was in the older part of the house, and we named it the Mother Hen Room. There was a queen-size bed and bunks where Mom could have all her chicks under her wings. About a year later, we built a honeymoon suite onto the back of the older part of the house. It was a very large unit. It was two levels and each level was 800 sq. ft. There was a spa in the garden room on the lower level. The upper part of the suite was decorated in peach and crème colors, using lots of lace. We preserved the real bird nest on the outer wall of the older part of house, and I put a pair of lovebirds in it. There was an attached screened-in porch where we served breakfast when the weather permitted. After we finished the honeymoon suite, we built a duplex up the hill from the main house. One side, the Dogwood Suite, had a kitchenette. The other side, the Redbud Suite, had a spa. Each unit was 600 sq. ft. There was a large porch across the front with rocking chairs.

Keith and I worked well together to do the cooking. He did the meat and eggs and I did the breads and fruits. We served a large country breakfast. Guests joked about how long they went after breakfast before being hungry enough to eat again. We had standard menus. The first day we served poached eggs on home-made biscuits with cheese sauce along with a meat. Orange juice, in-season fruit dishes, and quick breads were also served. Keith prided himself in his stuffed blueberry French toast that we would serve the second day or so. He made homemade bread in his breadmaker, dipped it in egg batter and grilled it. Inside was ricotta cheese and it was topped with blueberry syrup made with fresh blueberries from the Persimmon Hill Berry Farm located nearby. We cut the toast in triangles, put the back parts together to make the shape of a butterfly, and garnished the plate with real pansies. It was served with a meat and the usual juice, fruit, and quick bread or muffins. We had other menus as well, but these were two of the favorites. Guests liked our breakfasts!

A couple of events that happened while we had the B&B stand out in my mind. Keith had started teaching math at Reeds Spring, so during the school year, I did most of what had to be done at the B&B. On one occasion, we got a call at about 2 a.m. from the Redbud Suite that the lady staying there was ill and needed to go to the emergency room at the hospital. Our nearest hospital was in Berryville, Arkansas. I knew it would be very dif-ficult for them to find it alone, so I volunteered to drive and lead them to the hospital that was about fifteen miles away. I hurried and got dressed, grabbed the keys to the car, and started out the door. The last thing Keith said was, "Be careful and don't hit a deer." I got in the car as they started driving down from the suite to meet me. I backed up and hurt a loud, chilling *clunk!* I had backed into the car belonging to the folks staying in the honey-moon suite. I got out and looked, and sure enough, I had made a bad dent in their car. The gentleman who was taking his wife to the hospital said, "Did you hit the car?" "Yes," I said, "but let's go on, and I will take care of it when I get back."

I fretted and worried all the way to Berryville and back. How in the world was I going to tell our guests that I had run into their car? I was feeling sooo badly! I prayed and prayed about it. I got back home just as the sun was coming up. I hurried in the kitchen to fix breakfast, all the time wondering how I was going to tell our guests that I had hit their car and dented it.

The moment of truth came. The guests came in to breakfast and the good mornings were said. I took a deep breath and said, "Guys, I have something I have to tell you."

It was a serious moment. They looked at me waiting for the bad news.

"I ran into your car and dented it," I said. I prepared myself as much as possible for the anger I knew they would certainly express.

The gentleman said, "Oh, is that all? It's just metal. I thought you were going to tell us that we had to leave for some reason." He and his wife continued to reassure me that they were not that concerned. They felt that people were more important than things. What a wonderful example of Christian priority!

After breakfast, I phoned our insurance agent, and he came down from Springfield, took care of the business part, and all ended well.

We often had trouble with our chickens getting killed. If owls didn't get them, raccoons or neighbors' dogs were likely to. Keith built a big, tall fence around the chicken house and set a live animal trap.

While serving breakfast one morning, Charles came home from the College of the Ozarks in Hollister, Missouri, where he was attending. It was about thirty miles away, so he could run home fairly often. He came in the house very excited and asking, "Where's Dad?" He was about to burst out laughing. When he drove up into the yard, he looked down toward the chicken house and saw a skunk in Keith's live animal trap!

Now, how do you get a skunk out of a live trap? Very, very carefully! We went ahead and served breakfast while discussing what to do. The guests heard us talking and they thought it was funny.

After breakfast, Charles got Keith's fishing rod. He decided to cast a large hook and try to open the trap and let the skunk out gently before it spewed its scent. After a few casts, he hooked the trap. The guests, meanwhile, had gotten their video cameras and were recording the whole show. The door came open enough to let the skunk escape. Charles had gotten his rifle. He grabbed it and ran down behind the chicken house and shot the skunk out of site of the guests. Thankfully, we were spared the bad odor.

Trish had a beautiful wedding. She went to live with her husband in Colorado Springs where he was stationed in the military. David had joined the army before we left Denver. Kenneth and Charles were with us. We continued to improve the property. Winter came. Even though I had six homes under contract when we moved to Missouri, we were now having it rough financially. Keith's retirement was not big, and we didn't really have the business going strong yet. Charles was a junior in high school.

In January, Trish came to stay with us while her husband went on a field exercise with his army unit. She was pregnant. We had a good visit with her, and she went back to Colorado Springs when her husband got back from the exercise. They, too, were having a financially hard time. She applied for a temporary job and was assigned to unpack boxes coming in from overseas.

She said that there were bugs in the boxes of Christmas toys. On one occasion, a big, blue bug flew out of a box. The employees were all sent out of the room while it was fumigated. I now suggest to everyone that they wash things coming from overseas before using them. It was not pleasant to think of children playing with those toys on Christmas morning.

One day, we got a call from Trish. Keith answered the phone and reasoned that since she was calling collect, to save money, we would not accept the call but just call her back. When we called her back, we found her phone had been disconnected because they couldn't pay for it. Keith called the military base to talk to her husband. We found out that she had walked in subzero weather to a 7-Eleven store to phone us. The doctor had told her that she had preeclampsia and had to go to bed and stay on her right side until the baby came. We decided that I should go be with her.

I took a flight from Springfield and flew to Colorado Springs to be with her. They lived in a small apartment on the third floor of a large apartment complex. Trish could not work now, so finances were even tougher. The baby would be born on the post at the military hospital.

Since I had flown out, we had to share the one car. They had a little Ford Escort, and when her husband had slammed the door, the window in the door had broken. Trish and I took the Escort to get the window replaced and had to be careful that she didn't smell paint fumes while there. Even though she was supposed to be in bed, this had to be done. We got it replaced and felt better knowing that it wouldn't be so cold in that car.

While at their place, I slept on a leather loveseat, and their cat, named Elvis, kept stalking me! It would jump up on the back of the loveseat and walk slowly along. That was a bad cat! He would look mean at me. One time it jumped up on a hanging plant and knocked it down. It would walk on the top of the kitchen cabinets. I like cats, but this one was different. I worried about what it might do to the baby when it came. Her husband, Barry, was attached to it but finally said that we could get rid of it if we wouldn't tell him about it. Before the baby came, we talked a nurse into taking it.

I spent most of the time knitting for the baby. I was concerned that we had no way to get to the hospital during the day in case of emergency since they had only the one vehicle, and her husband had to take it to the base. I was relieved, actually, when the doctor said she should go to the hospital. I would ride out with Barry in the mornings and stay with her all day. She was in the hospital three weeks and then they decided to induce labor and take the baby.

They took her to a room off the labor room and began the intravenous medication. She began having labor pains but nothing really happened. As it turned out, it was not until late the next day that she delivered. I stayed with her and slept in the "catapult" recliner in the room. (Every time I sat up, the chair quickly jumped up and almost shot me out of it, so I said it was like a catapult.) While she was waiting, they were wheeling other mothers-to-be past her room. Most were screaming and yelling. One father lost it! He was yelling as loud as he could, "Breathe!" I thought, "That was one Lamaze lesson that didn't really get across as to the purpose of a father being by the mother's side!"

Finally, the time came to take Trish into the delivery room. The doctor and nurse asked me to go with her. I checked with Barry and her to see what they wanted, and they did want me to go in with her. We donned our white garbs and in we went. There were three doctors on hand. When the baby came out, its head was cone-shaped. One doctor assured me that it would not remain that way. The nurse started writing on the chart. "Now, let's see." she said, "She is type A positive blood type, isn't she?" I couldn't believe what I was hearing. Almost every day they had drawn blood. In the very first doctor's visit, Trish had mentioned to the doctor that she was type A negative, and that we were concerned about the Rh factor. The nurse told me that the chart showed her as type A positive. They had to draw blood again to see for sure while she was lying there on the delivery table. Sure enough, she was type A negative.

The baby began to turn blue. The doctors and nurses scurried around faster. They took him away quickly. I stayed with Trish. They wheeled her into the recovery room. They inserted a catheter in her. We knew something was wrong with the baby, but we didn't know what it was. I had walked around the room where they were keeping the baby and peered through the windows several times to check on him. There was a needle stuck in his head and other needles and tubes on him also. They finally told me to quit coming around.

Soon, the doctor came in her room and said, "The baby is not breathing right. We've decided to transport him by ambulance across town to the neonatal center in case he goes sour on us." I couldn't believe my ears! To think that a doctor would use those words to a young couple! As soon as he left the room, I asked the kids if they wanted to have prayer. We joined hands and I led in prayer. It was decided that Barry would follow the ambulance to the other hospital. He left the room, but soon came back. He was crying and said, "I just can't do it." I went downstairs and watched as they loaded the little guy into the back of the ambulance. It was one of the hardest things I have ever done. The tears were welling up in my eyes, and I began to sniffle. Trying to hide my sorrow, as soon as the ambulance drove away, I went back to Trish.

Soon, another doctor, a specialist from the neonatal hospital, phoned her and asked her a series of questions related to her pregnancy. She felt better knowing that someone cared enough to phone her. One of the questions he asked was whether she had been by a wood-burning stove. We never knew the true significance of that while remembering that we had the wood-burning stove in our family room, and she had been there quite a bit.

As it turned out, the baby was in intensive care for eight days while Trish remained in the hospital a couple of weeks. They pumped Trish's breasts, froze the milk, and took it to the other hospital. Trish took the whole thing better than I did. How hard it must have been for her to have her newborn baby miles away and not be able to get to him while she, herself, needed care.

The daughter of the Nazarene missionary we had known at Ramah was living in Colorado Springs. She would drive me to the hospital almost every day to see the baby, who by now had been named Dylan. She had worked at that hospital at one time and was familiar with it. She told me about all the little drug babies that ended up there. It was strange to look at Dylan, weighing over eight pounds, in the incubator beside the other incubators with tiny, tiny babies. I overheard some adults telling about how their doctor's bill was over $100,000. One little baby was jerking because its mother had been on drugs. It was my understanding that most of the babies there were having problems related to the mother having used drugs. For the first time, I was tempted to think that abortion for these babies might have been better. Poor little things were suffering because of what their mommies had done. It wasn't fair! Of course, it was wrong to think that abortion should be acceptable. The girl who was driving me to the hospital told me several stories about how those little babies they had cared for there had grown up to be successful citizens. In fact, she said that they would have a time to bring babies back on their tenth birthdays to see them and realize how healthy they were.

On the third day in the incubator, Dylan actually rolled over from his tummy to his back. He was creeping from one end of the incubator to the other. It was apparent that he was a fighter, and I began to believe that he would make it. Trish wondered why I hadn't shown a lot of positive emotion to him. Truth was that I was afraid to get too attached for fear he wouldn't make it.

In the meantime, while Trish was in the hospital, the lease was up on their apartment, and they had no place to go. As she lay in the hospital bed, she circled ads in the newspaper of places for rent. She made calls from her hospital bed and found a place. The next problem was how to get them moved. Barry was not allowed to take leave. I talked to the hospital chaplain. How I appreciated him! He talked to some of his friends, they got a truck, and they moved everything to the other place. When Trish and Dylan were finally released from the hospitals, they went to the new place. What another emotional challenge for a young mother! She couldn't even go back to her other apartment.

I had scrubbed and scrubbed that first apartment so they could get their deposit back. I got on my hands and knees and used toothpicks to clean around the molding. I cleaned the stove until it was shining. They were sure to get their deposit back! However, the manager of the apartment said it was not acceptable and refused to refund the deposit. A lesson was learned. There is a good chance that apartment owners and managers won't give the deposit back no matter how clean the place is. That is a source of income the many owners plan to keep.

I was glad the new place was on ground level. Dylan still needed special care and instructions were given to Barry and Trish about how to start him breathing again if he should stop.

About three days after Trish was released, she got really sick, and we had to get her back to the hospital. She had bladder and urinary tract infection. She had told me the night Dylan was born, "Mom, they have the catheter tube looped over the bed rail. If they don't change it, the urine will back up and cause infection." I had gotten the nurse to change it, but apparently the damage was already done. That time, it was necessary for her to take antibiotic, and she finally got better.

Things finally smoothed out, and I went back home. I had gone out to be with her right after Valentine's Day. Dylan was born April 5. It was quite an ordeal for all of us. As soon as I was able, I sent a small check along with my heartfelt thanks to the chaplain who had helped us so much. It was a real lesson to me that at some time or another, most of us may need to depend on someone else.

I am happy to say that at this writing, Dylan is twenty-three years old and doing great. He is over six feet tall and weighs over two hundred pounds. He graduated from high school with almost a semester of college hours. We had been told that he might have trouble with his eyes and that he might be mentally retarded. He does wear contacts, but both his mother and I are nearsighted as he is, so it is probably natural. He always made good grades and is an especially wonderful person. He still has a white streak in his hair where the needle was stuck in his soft spot. It is a reminder to us of how good God is to have helped us through all of that. Looking back, however, I think it was too much for Barry to handle. When he got out of the military, and they moved to Chicago to be near his folks, Dylan got sick with pneumonia, and they ended up with a big hospital bill. They had a really hard time. Barry was working nights and trying to watch

Dylan during the day while Trish worked. Trish became pregnant again and had absolutely no trouble when LeAndra was born. When Dylan was five and LeAndra was three, Barry told Trish that he wanted a divorce. He left them, and Trish has shown exceptional courage through the years as she has raised two wonderful children and has become outstanding in her career. Dylan and LeAndra are both in college. LeAndra is in the top 15 percent of the college of engineering at UNLV (University of Nevada, Las Vegas) majoring in civil engineering. Dylan is majoring in international business.

When I got home from Colorado Springs, we hurried to get ready for summer guests at the B and B. I signed us up with Kanakuk Kamp in their list of places for parents to stay when they checked out their children. God blessed us and we had a good year. We had decided that we would always have Keith lead the prayer before serving breakfast. On more than one occasion, we would go to the table to have prayer, and the guests would already have their heads bowed and would be saying their own prayer. When I was in real estate, I had given a Bible to my clients at each closing. I decided to give a Bible to each guest family at the B and B. God was blessing us with wonderful people as guests. It was a true joy.

Since we were still having trouble adjusting to living on a retirement check, I decided to try to teach. I applied for a teaching job but found that I would need to take several hours of college to qualify in Missouri. One day the phone rang, and it was the principal of the Shell Knob School. He asked me if I would be interested in teaching GED since I would be qualified to teach in that program. This started my now twentieth year of teaching GED (Adult Education and Literacy). I taught two nights a week. I talked to my supervisor and told her that I thought we should start a class at Blue Eye, too. She hired Keith as my assistant at Shell Knob and hired me to assist Keith in teaching at Blue Eye. We were teaching four nights a week which worked out fine. This gave us some winter income, albeit not very much.

Keith, in the meantime, had been applying for teaching jobs. No one wanted to hire him because he was too qualified and experienced and would be too high on the pay scale. Most schools wanted to hire teachers in step one on the scale right out of college.

I was sitting at the dining table one day and looking at the paper. I noticed an ad for a math teacher at Reeds Spring. As it turned out, the teacher had left in the middle of the year, and they were having a hard time finding a replacement. Keith was hired, but they would not give him credit for all of his experience and education. He taught during the day, and I took care of the bed and breakfast. I taught at night at both places, and he took care of the bed and breakfast at night. It worked out fine and things began to look up.

We had moved to the farm in 1988 and sold it in 2005. God blessed us all the time we were there. It had become a year-round business. We gave discounts during the off-season to college students from the two Bible colleges in Springfield. They would sometimes come down for a weekend to relax. Each year, more and more people came because they had heard of us by word of mouth, so our advertising expense dropped to almost nothing.

We felt sad when we got to the point that we just couldn't handle all of the work anymore. It was difficult to get help. We just needed part-time help. Retired people who knew how to clean didn't want to work that hard. Teenagers wanted the work, but required a lot of training. Others wanted full-time work and would usually find jobs in Branson. Keith retired from teaching and soon found that he had diabetes. I began to deal with arthritis and had to have bone spurs removed from the heel of one foot and later had knee trouble. We knew what we had to do. Again, God worked everything out in His timing, and we sold the farm after fifteen good years. It was a good time to sell, and we made a good profit.

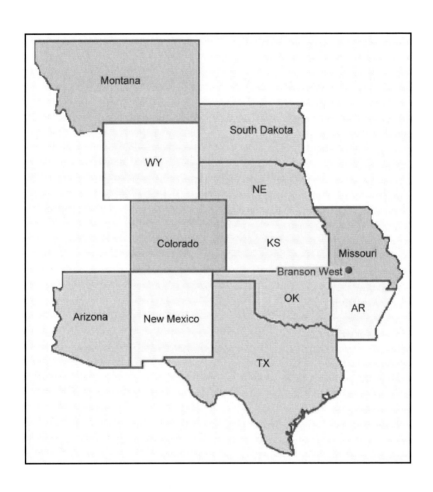

The Sunset is Beautiful

Branson West, Missouri

We now have a home overlooking Table Rock Lake in Branson West, Missouri. We are enjoying the sunset of our lives in a home nicer than we ever dreamed we would have. "What a nice place to be homebound," my husband commented after his recent stay in the hospital.

Again, God was visible in his working in our lives. After about fifteen years of successfully running the B and B, we realized we were no longer able to keep up with the work. We tried to sell a few years earlier, but it didn't work out. God had other plans.

When Keith found he had diabetes, and I had to have bone spurs removed from my foot, we had to face the fact that B and B time was over. We officially put the farm on the market with a very patient young lady realtor. She showed us many, many places, and we put offers on two of them only to find they had sold before our offers could be considered. Our farm went under contract, and we still did not have a place to go.

I had not asked for prayer from our little church because I felt that they might pray that we wouldn't leave. Finally, on a Wednesday evening at prayer meeting I asked for prayer. Immediately the pastor said, "We'll pray that you don't leave!" I explained that that had been the reason prayer had not been asked for earlier. Then, they seriously prayed that we would find the right place.

The next morning, we again went with our patient young realtor to look at houses. The first one we looked at was the right one! We both felt comfortable in the house, and we knew it was the one!

There are many beautiful houses in the world, but ours is the most beautiful and appropriate for us! How often we have thought of how we were willing to go on the reservation and live in a hogan. God had rewarded us for our willingness by giving us special, lovely homes to enjoy. He is so wonderful!

I am again teaching GED, and still enjoy it. The experiences I have had in teaching GED classes could possibly fill a book by themselves! During the time I have taught these classes, I have experienced hearing of the deaths of four students. There are many tragic stories associated with the students I have tried to help. Keith served four years on the school board at Reeds Spring. We try to help out at the church we attend. I teach the senior ladies in Sunday school and Keith serves as a deacon. I am writing a weekly column titled, "Train up a Child" for some of the local newspapers. I have published two books, *Let the Children Come* and *Children, Come to Me*. They are books of weekly lessons for children based on Scripture. I am also writing a column about raising children for *The Pathway*, the paper published by the Missouri Baptist Convention.

At this writing, Kenneth is the managing director for a non-profit in Washington State. His organization partners with the Indian Health Service and offers training, support, and facilitation for the introduction of rapid HIV testing into the existing universal screening programs for the health clinics of six different tribes. Trish lives in Chino Hills, California, where she served as vice president of the Southwest region for a major insurance company until a merger was made with another company that cost her the job. She is currently employed by another major insurance company in the workman's compensation division. Now that her children are grown, she is pursuing her law degree. Our youngest son, Charles, is married and has two little boys, Garrett, age eight, and Spencer, age two. He is plant manager for a large beef plant in Grand Island, Nebraska. His wife, Kelly, is a great homemaker and very capable in a number of areas.

On what would have been David's forty-sixth birthday, we received the sad news that he had passed away. He is buried in Spring River Cemetery in Verona, where we have purchased eight grave plots for Keith and I and any family members who may need them. The family was together for the funeral at our lake home in Branson West. Amidst the sadness of our loss, there was also a pride in the other children, and how the love for one another was shining through. Each of the other children displayed responsible behavior and understanding of the seriousness of life itself.

David had served in the army as a driver of an M1-A1 tank. He had been well-named, as it turned out, as he was the warrior of the family. I often thought of him as being like King David in the Bible who was a real warrior. He had always been interested in WWII and other wars. Although we had never had alcohol in the home, David died as an alcoholic. He apparently had started drinking after leaving home. From our experience working with the American Indian people, we knew that alcohol was a real problem among the Indian people. I had always cautioned both Kenneth and David to never take the first drink lest they become addicted. David told me during his last days, "Mom, I am so ashamed. I never thought it would happen to me." He had broken the addiction of cigarettes by sheer will power and had always been a very determined person. I kept hoping against hope that he could overcome the hold of alcohol, but on that sad day, I answered the door to find a uniformed law officer. I jokingly said, "What did we do wrong?" He solemnly answered, "Nothing, Maam. May I come in?" He had the bad news for us that David had been found in his trailer in Aurora, Illinois. His heart had given out.

David was gifted with the use of words. He loved to do creative writing. Here are two of his poems which he wrote while attending Haskell Indian University in Lawrence, Kansas. It is my understanding that they were published there with other creative writings of the students.

A Last Prayer

Child warrior, why have you so meekly knelt?
A plea, common with your breed.
I know why your heart thunders silently.

Soft as breath of a newborn does your plea rise like the dew on an early morning.
You are troubled by the symbols that you carry—Uncertain the feeling about your return.

Child warrior, your plea is unheld by the walls that house you.
Destiny is an open scroll, waiting to hold your everlasting courage.

The Pack Rat

He's so cautious, which is crucial for the moment.
Like a small child the packrat innocently steals.

Slight of hand like a blink of an eye does the pack rat
Take a tiny treasure which is vague to many
Deeply fills a venturous heart with glee.

≈

Impulse, or nature, that prods the culprit and how quietly
Does the pack rat commit his crystal crime again.

—David Lamb

David reviewed some of the writing of this book and was
my constant encourager to get me started writing. I may have
never written a book had it not been for his prodding. He is
greatly missed!

Keith and I had phoned David that morning and when
we didn't get an answer, we had gone ahead and sung "Happy
Birthday" to him, not realizing that he was already gone from
this world.

When we adopted Kenneth and David, it was our hope that
we were leading them to a life with Christ, and that someday,
they would perhaps become missionaries to the American Indian
people. I had always told our children that God had a plan for
their lives. At first, I felt that David had not lived out the plan
God had for him. Our daughter, Trish, said, "Mom, maybe he did
live out the plan God had for him. I could never have made it
without Dave's help. He was a help to all of us." (David lived with
Trish and paid rent for a number of years. He was a great help to
her after her husband left.)

David had worked ten years for Insurance Auto Auction after
leaving the army. I know that one of the stages of grief is blame. I
had visions of truck drivers taking him out for a drink and laughing at the drunk Indian. He told me once that some people at
work had called him "chief," and he didn't like to have to put up
with that.

David's caregiver, Francine O'Conner, at Hines Veteran's
Hospital was a big help to us during the last months of David's
life. She was a real answer to prayer. She seemed so concerned
about David and kept us informed of his treatment and actions.

I cannot praise her enough. She kept in constant contact with us knowing that we were unable to be with him. It was as though she were a surrogate mother to him. I could tell by her voice that she grew to have a special affection for Dave as did so many other people. It has been a little more than a year at this writing since we said good-bye to him, and just this week, we got a card from her letting us know she was thinking of us. I hope to meet this wonderful woman, dubbed "Florence Nightingale" by David, someday in heaven, if not before.

❧

The question remains. Was the effort made during our lives like mere whispers in the wind? Did our words go unheard? Did our efforts have no effect? I don't think so. Admittedly, there were times when we felt as though all of our efforts were just "blown away" and that there was no lasting value in what we were doing or had done. Through the years, a real truth has been revealed. We are not judged by results, but rather by our love for and closeness to our Maker. That love produces effort. Effort for Christ is a visible proof of love for him. As God looks down on each of us, He wants love for Him more than anything. The results of the efforts we have made are in His hands! There are many Christian people who perhaps feel as we have felt at times. Living a commonplace life with little recognition does not mean that our efforts are unimportant in God's sight. We make a mistake when we judge our work by whether or not we become famous or are recognized as important. We are not responsible for results, but only for our efforts. Someone once said that if we please God, it doesn't matter who we displease, and, if we displease God, it doesn't matter who we please. God alone knows whether our lives have produced only whispers in the wind or more.

As King Solomon said:

> Now all has been heard;
> here is the conclusion of

the matter:
Fear God and keep His
commandments,
for this is the whole duty of man.
For God will bring every
deed into judgment,
including every hidden
thing,
whether it is good or evil.

Ecclesiastes 12:13 and 14 (NIV)

The statue of the WWI soldier still stands guard at the end of Main Street in Verona. It is a testimony to the patriotism of the community.

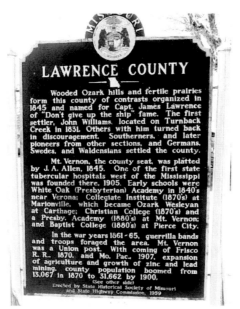

Verona has an interesting history as related on this sign near the statue in Verona Park.

The pictured monument is placed on the site near the head of Spring River to show the location of the first Sunday School west of the Mississippi River and south of the Missouri River. As a child, my friends and I played on the remains of the old log school.

The "trap door" on the steeple of the Catholic church in Verona is barely visible as a dark spot about halfway to the top. It served as a good discipline tool for my sister who told my younger sister and I that the priest would come and get us and throw us out that door if we didn't behave. I thought of this in later years on the Navajo Reservation when we found out about the legend of Spider Woman. The methods of discipline were similar.

The old Lechner and Haddock grocery stores are still standing side by side in Verona. The son of the owner of the Lechner store on the right later became my brother-in-law.

These items were found while Keith and some of the boys from his dorm were hiking near Lukachukai. They had been placed a certain way in a particular place by a medicine man.

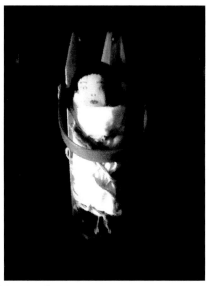

A Navajo couple gave this to us as a going-away gift when we left Lukachukai. "Since you have no children of your own, we made you a baby," they said.

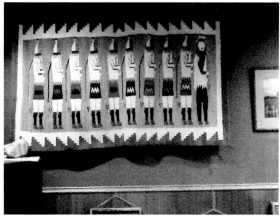

Navajo rug depicting a yea-be-chi dance. The leader is the "grandmother". Faintly detectable is the white spirit line on the lower righthand corner. When a rug had borders, it was thought that a spirit line was necessary to let out the evil spirits. The rock shown in the lower lefthand corner is an ancient axe head.

These three paintings were done by students at Albuquerque Indian School when Keith was superintendent there. The painting on the left depicts a ceremony of the Native Church of North America. We were told that at these meetings, participants are able to talk directly to Jesus and can hear whispers across the room. We were also told that participants of this religion generally do not have a problem with alcohol. The peyote used in the ceremonies comes from a cactus found in Texas.

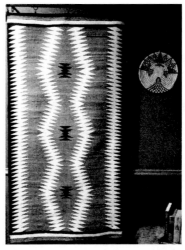

Navajo rug made by Edith Garcia and her mother and given to us as a Christmas gift. Edith babysat and cleaned for us while I taught school at Ramah, NM.

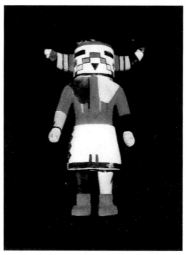

Kachina dolls were made by the Hopi Indians. We took cottonwood to a man at one of the villages to trade for Kachina dolls.

Dragonflies and frogs represent the cycle of life on this pot from Zuni pueblo.

This pot was given to Keith by a lady at Jemez pueblo to show her appreciation for his work there while he was educational administrator for the southern pueblos. She made it herself.

Pictured are items used in the Native Church of North America. The leather pouch holds peyote, a drug legalized for use in worship.

A Hopi Indian man made this drum for us in exchange for several cottonwood logs we took to him.

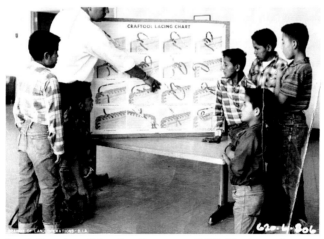

At Cutbank Boarding School in Browning, MT., Keith taught some of the boys in the dormitory how to do leathercrafting.

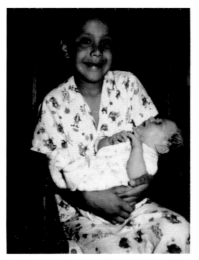

When Trish, our daughter was born, Kenneth and David were overjoyed. This is a picture of Kenneth holding her when we brought her home from the hospital.

This picture was taken of our family in the early 1970's. Our youngest son, Charles, was born in 1973. Keith was the youngest superintendent of a school in the Bureau of Indian Affairs at the time.

Dylan and LeAndra, our grandchildren, spent most summers with us and helped us at Grandpa's Farm B & B. At this writing, Dylan is in college working on his business degree. LeAndra attends UNLV and is majoring in civil engineering.

One activity we did at the Bed and Breakfast was a community old-fashioned pig roast. Everyone who dressed in old-fashioned clothing got to eat beans and cornbread free. We served that along with sassafras tea and Amish Friendship Bread. The original part of the Bed and Breakfast was built in 1892-93 of hand-hewn limestone. We were told that the builder was paid 2 cows, 2 horses, and a pig. Pictured are Keith and I in our old-fashioned clothes in front of our Hillside Hideaway.

Our grandchildren, Dylan and LeAndra, stayed with us most summers as they were growing up and helped us at Grandpa's Farm Bed and Breakfast. They were baptized in King's River near Carr Lane, MO. They were a big help to us at the B & B.

The Ozark region is a wonderful place to enjoy life's sunset. This picture is taken from our deck overlooking Table Rock Lake. Silver Dollar City is on the far hill. It is one of the biggest attractions in Branson, MO.

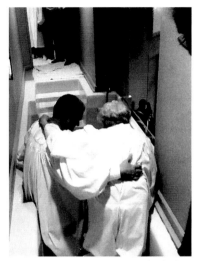

Wilma Markette, a lady in the senior ladies Life Group that I teach, is getting baptized by our pastor, Jeff Hardy. Wilma is eighty-nine years old.

Our oldest son, Kenneth, has participated for the last three years in a tree decorating charity event in Bellingham, WA. He has been a ribbon winner each year. He currently works for a non-profit involving tribes in the Northwest.

Our daughter lives in CA. She is a single mom of two college students. She is pictured here in her office where she was recently employed.

Our youngest son, Charles, is now a father of two little boys. He stands proudly with his dad in the house they lived in in Iowa. After they moved, a tornado blew the house completely down and blew his shop away.

Our daughter-in-law often serves as a source of information for my column "Train up a child" that appears in local newspapers. She certainly has plenty of opportunities to keep in tune with modern day challenges in raising children as she and our son, Charles, train up Garrett on the left and Spencer on the right.

"Our granddaughter, LeAndra, hard at work in Las Vegas. She is majoring in civil engineering at University of Nevada in Las Vegas."

Our oldest son, Kenneth, designed the funeral announcement for David and put the military picture and this picture of when he was a child on the announcement with the two poems printed in this book that David had written while attending Haskell Indian University.

Our second son, David, drove a tank in the army. After leaving the army, he settled in Aurora, IL., and we were notified on his 46th birthday that he had been found deceased.

David's remains are in Spring River Cemetery in Verona, MO. When Trish, our daughter, came with Dylan and LeAndra, our grandchildren, to visit from CA, we each placed a rose on the grave in remembrance.